Excel at Interviews

Patricia McBride is a management and inter-personal skills trainer. Formerly a senior social worker, she moved on to having responsibility for training 650 social services staff. From there Patricia gradually moved into a more business-orientated environment and for three years she was a director of a busy business-training company. Today she provides independent training and consultancy services to businesses, Cambridge University and local authorities.

Patricia has wide experience running both public and in-company courses. Subjects include selection- and appraisal-interviewing skills, staff management topics, assertion-training, planning for retirement and stress management. One of her courses, 'Staff Management Skills' has received NEBS certification. She is also a freelance journalist.

Patricia's previous publications include:

- *The Positive Approach*, a CRAC training manual enabling teachers to run assertion-training courses for 14–17 year-olds. Hobsons.

- *How to Interview*, a training manual for those teaching selection-interviewing techniques

- *How to Get that Job*, a training manual for those teaching job-seeking skills

- *Study Skills for Success*, a book to help 13–16 year-olds improve their study skills. Hobsons.

- *CVs and Applications*, a book for job seekers aged 16–21. Hobsons.

Excel at Interviews

Tactics for job and college applicants

Patricia McBride

Student Helpbook Series

HOBSONS

CRAC

2nd Edition

Acknowledgments

I would like to thank the following people for giving their time and assistance in writing this book: Doreen Dace, Rachel Dace, Helen Coffey, Patricia Duckworth, Lorraine Kaka, Jeanette Hurworth, Julie Digby, Tina Bowen, Linde Raisbeck, Sam Lavender, Yasmin Sherratt, Julie Digby.

Also, thanks to the Commission for Racial Equality and the Equal Opportunities Commission for allowing me to reproduce material from their leaflets.

 © Hobsons Publishing PLC, 1993, 1995

ISBN 1 86017 097 8

CRAC

The Careers Research and Advisory Centre (CRAC) is a registered educational charity. Hobsons Publishing PLC produces CRAC publications under exclusive licence and royalty agreements.

Printed and bound in Great Britain by Clays Ltd, Bungay, Suffolk.

Ref. L258/ss/8/qq/E/JF

Contents

Introduction

1 Interview Preparation

2 The Successful Interview

3 After the Interview

How to Use this Helpbook

This Helpbook will be of use to anyone who is at or beyond the application stage in looking for:

- → a job, or
- → a place at college or university.

Although these may seem like very different outcomes, their application processes have many things in common:

- → the need to think ahead to what you really want
- → the need to conduct a successful interview
- → the need to review your performance for future interviews

There are, of course, some differences as well. For this reason, sections of some chapters are appropriate to one or the other. However, most of the information will apply to both. Either way, this Helpbook will guide you through the whole interview process: the preparation; the interview itself; and afterwards. You will find case-studies, quotes, examples, and checklists to make you think long and hard about how you approach the interview situation. It will also give you lots of information and improve your confidence in your ability to perform.

Selling yourself

At any interview, whether for a college place or a job, you are selling a product and that product is *you*. So for a minute imagine you are on a sales course. What advice would you be given? Well, here are some guidelines in books I've looked at:

Analyse your market – know where to look for courses and jobs.

Know your product – that's you. You should know yourself a lot better by the end of this book.

Study your customer – that's your interviewer(s).

Have a positive attitude – this book includes ways to keep calm during an interview.

The psychology of selling – we'll look at what makes interviewers tick.

Buying motives – we'll also consider what interviewers are looking for.

Body language – very important. This books considers both yours and the interviewer's body language.

How to overcome objections – how to get round those awkward questions.

Closing the sale – ensuring you get the offer you want.

So there you have it! That's pretty much the topics we'll be working through in this book to help you succeed at one of your most important sales pitches.

I have been 'sold to' by many people for both college places and jobs. I have also been teaching courses for people attending interviews for some time now, but, even more to the point, I have taught courses for managers who want to know how to interview, so I know what they're looking for. This Helpbook will give you all the little tricks and know-how to succeed. (Mind you, I teach the interviewers what the little tricks are too, so hope that you don't get any of them interviewing you . . .)

How this book is organised

This book is in three distinct parts – before, during and after the interview. Each chapter starts with a brief summary of what is covered and at what stage of the interview process to read the chapter. If you spend a few minutes reading through these summaries before you read anything else, you will be able to use your time effectively. There is also a checklist at the end of each chapter that acts as a useful revision aid or quick reference.

You will probably not want or need to read through the whole book in one go, although it would certainly be helpful if you could do so. The point is to use the book in the way that is most useful to you.

You can learn a lot from reading how to do something, but even more from actually doing it. For this reason, there are a number of exercises in the book. These exercises are designed to get you thinking hard about yourself in relation to the interview process. Please do not feel that you have to do every exercise. Choose those exercises which cover areas where you need to improve your skills or self-awareness.

Your interview file

To help you make the most of this book and your chances at interview, I suggest that you get yourself a file of some sort (ring-binder or envelope). You will need to keep in the file:

- details of each job or course you apply for
- copies of application forms or CVs you've sent out (Don't forget to take copies of them – they'll save time when filling in the next one and help your interview preparation.)
- your answers to the exercises in this book
- your record of how well you did in your mock interview
- your review sheets to follow each interview

But before we look in detail at interview techniques, here are the experiences of three people who have already been through the interview process. Their stories will highlight the great variety of ways in which interviews are conducted.

Tina's Story

' I went for an interview for my first job when I was still at school. The job was a Youth Training placement, working for a district council. I would be work-shadowing and would get day-release to do a course on one day a week over a year, which was the equivalent to a two-year full-time course in college, and, of course, I'd be getting paid. Other than that, I didn't know much about the job or the place before I went and so I didn't really know if I even wanted it.

'The college said my mum had to take me to the interview and I was really glad, because I felt more confident with her there. Even so, I was really nervous. I was expecting the interview to be really formal and strict, like school. Our school didn't give us much idea what to expect.

'I had a letter telling me where to go, and that bit was all straightforward. When one of the interviewers came to get me, she was enormous, absolutely huge – I felt completely overpowered. She took me into a tiny interview room and the other interviewer was nearly as big! They seemed to fill the room. They sat some distance away from each other so it was difficult to keep them both in view at the same time. We sat in low comfortable chairs in a triangle with me nearest the door. Ready to make an escape if necessary!

'Still, I needn't have been so nervous; they quickly made me feel relaxed. In fact, they were much more human and understanding than the interviewer who I saw for a place in college.

'They seemed to do most of the talking. They told me all about the district council and that I would be able to try working in different departments. I was really excited about this, especially when they said I could try working in Personnel – something I really wanted to do.

'I can't remember many of the questions they asked. I

don't think they asked many. I do remember though that they asked me what I wanted to do in the future and how I thought I'd do in my exams. They told me I'd only be offered the place if my exam results were okay.

'For part of the interview, one of them went outside and spoke to my mum while the other one chatted to me. I don't know what she asked my mum.

'That was it really. They shook my hand and showed me out. I left determined to work even harder at my exams so that I could go to work there.

'I got the place and loved the job, especially working with the large lady who turned out to be really good fun!

Rachel's Story

I was invited to an interview for a place at a big London college to do a maths degree. I hadn't been for an interview before, so I was a bit unsure exactly what to expect. We were told to arrive by 11.30 am – everyone who was being interviewed that day arrived at the same time, about 20 of us. Everyone was smartly dressed and some people were wearing suits.

'First of all we were led to a lecture theatre where the admissions tutor gave us a talk about the college, courses, scholarships, etc. The tutor said that they were interviewing 300 people for 100 places. We were told that some existing students would be hanging around to chat so that we could ask questions informally. In fact, that was great. They had about one student to every three applicants, so we all got a chance to ask anything we wanted very informally. The students sat with us at lunch too, and so did some of the tutors. It was very casual and quite relaxed.

'After lunch, a couple of the students took us on a tour of the whole college – lecture rooms, study areas, living accommodation, the lot. That was really helpful, because we could ask all sorts of things about college life that we probably wouldn't have thought of during the interview. The students who took us round were very chatty and jokey, so it felt okay.

'After the tour, we went to a lecture theatre and one of the lecturers gave us a 20-minute lecture. He said he wanted to point out that maths at degree level was quite different from A-level maths. And it was. He did some applied maths, with a bucket and some water. It was really interesting. We were encouraged to ask questions and he asked us some during a discussion session that followed the lecture. This wasn't part of the selection procedure itself. I found it really interesting and it made me look forward even more to studying the subject.

'Some people went straight from there to their interviews, but I had the last interview of the day so I went with some of the others to have tea. Some of the people who had finished their interview came in to speak to us before they left. They told us it was awful. (It wasn't!) The interviewers came to collect us from there. I was interviewed by only one person, although I know that some of the others had two interviewers.

'My interviewer, a male lecturer (who was wearing a suit and tie), was very friendly as we walked towards his room. He asked about my journey, the weather and told me his son went to college in Cambridge, which is where I live. It was more formal when we got to his room. He had a chair on either side of a table and he sat one side and I sat the other.

'He started off by telling me about the course, then asked me why I had chosen to do it and why I wanted to go to that particular college. Actually, it was my second choice of college, but I didn't tell him that. I'm interested in music and want to make that my career in the end, so I told him I was interested in the college because as well as the course being what I was looking for, it had good music facilities and was near a major centre for music.

'One thing I wasn't expecting – he gave me a sort of applied maths test. He suddenly produced a pen and paper, drew a diagram and started asking me questions about it. It wasn't too difficult, and he helped me out, but I think the main thing that he was trying to find out was how my mind worked.

'After that he asked me about the courses I'd done at school, and I actually had to give a brief summary of what I thought I'd learnt in some of them. Then he asked me how much time I had for leisure activities and what I liked to do (apart from music, which he already knew). He made it fairly easy to speak because he seemed interested in what I was saying.

'He got out the reference from my head teacher and read it through. Presumably he had read it before. He had certainly read my UCAS form because I could see he'd highlighted bits of it with a marker pen.

'After all that, he told me straight away what their offer would be and that I would get written confirmation to follow. Then he showed me to the door and off I went.

'My tips to people would be to keep calm (I do the Alexander Technique to help my body posture when I'm playing the viola, and this helps me to keep relaxed), and to really know about the course and the college, and current affairs related to the course you're applying for. Also, be honest, be yourself, don't make things up.'

Sam's Story

'I recently had an interview for a place on an English and American literature degree course in a college in the Midlands.

'Our sixth-form college is pretty good about interviews and one of the teachers gave me a mock interview the day before. He told me he would be really mean during the interview and he was. It was very good practice (and the interview wasn't nearly so bad).

'I travelled to the Midlands by coach and got off at the wrong town! I had to quickly get a train the rest of the way. Luckily, I had allowed plenty of time and still got there okay.

'Before the interview, prospective students were shown round the whole college in groups of four, each group being escorted by two first-year students. It was good, we got a chance to get to know each other and chat as we walked round. The college was very impressive, I liked it. After the tour, we were given a cup of tea in the common room while we waited for our interview. We were all a bit nervous and as we were all applying for the same course we kept asking each other the sort of questions we thought the interviewer might ask.

'I was interviewed by a lecturer from the course. She took me to her office, and we sat on a couple of comfortable chairs. The desk was against the wall, not between us. I think I had been expecting two hard chairs and a bright light shining in my face! She was very friendly and informal. She asked me first about my journey, and I told her the problems I'd had. A stroke of luck was that she used to teach at my school some time ago, and knew one of the teachers quite well. We spent about ten minutes talking about that.

'After the more informal bit, she began to ask me about my A-levels. As I said, I had been very worried that I wouldn't be able to answer some questions, so I had done a lot of preparation. I had spent time noting ten points I wanted to get across and also thought about how I could make links between the A-level subjects I had chosen as well as between the different books I had been reading for English A-level. I was determined to have some say in the way the interview went. Also, I was worried that I might get asked questions on American literature and I wanted to avoid that because I haven't read any . . .

'Actually, I needn't have worried. I was expecting a succession of questions thrown at me so rapidly that I wouldn't have time to think, but there was plenty of time to talk about each question, and none were really tough. We talked about English literature and I managed to keep quite a lot of control of the interview by thinking ahead to what questions she might ask about what I was saying. This meant I could say things like "Well, you might think . . .", and go on to give a reasoned argument for what I was saying. Not that she made it difficult. She encouraged me to keep speaking by nodding and saying things like "And what else do you think?" In fact, a couple of times the conversation seemed so easy that I wondered if I was being overbearing because I was doing all the talking, so I stopped and said "What do you think?"

'We also talked about high and popular culture, including a couple of programmes on television at the moment. Fortunately I'd seen them both. One is an adaptation of a book we're reading for A-level and we discussed different aspects of that. Really, I could forget it was an interview. It seemed like chatting to a friend about a subject we were both interested in.

'At the end of the interview, she asked me if I had any questions. I had a couple prepared ahead of time and asked her those.

'I don't know yet if I'll be offered a place, but she was speaking as if I would. I really enjoyed the interview and feel much more self-confident now that I've been through one.

'My advice to anyone facing an interview would be to decide what points you want to make and try to think of all the objections the interviewer may think of. That way you can pre-empt them. Make sure you get the chance to talk about the things you want to cover, but admit if you don't know something. Your mind shouldn't ever go blank if you've done enough preparation.'

1

Interview Preparation

1 Mental Preparation

You should read this chapter:

- ➤➤ as soon as you begin thinking about applying for a job or college place. It will also be of help when you are completing an application form or your CV
- ➤➤ if you are preparing for a specific interview

By the end of this chapter you should know:

- ➤➤ what interviewers are looking for in candidates
- ➤➤ how to evaluate your skills
- ➤➤ the format of a typical interview
- ➤➤ how to use background material to help you prepare for the interview
- ➤➤ how to present facts in the most favourable way
- ➤➤ how interviewers 'score' candidates
- ➤➤ questioning techniques used by interviewers

Interviews! Does anybody like them? Most of us would answer this with a resounding 'NO!', but believe it or not there are people who actually enjoy interviews. They have an unusual attitude towards the whole thing. Unlike us mere mortals who see interviews as about as inviting as a visit to the dentist, these curious people see them as a two-way process, an opportunity to find out whether they want the job or the college place as well as a chance for the interviewer to find out if they want them. Not only that, they like having a chance to talk about themselves! Very strange. However, with the right preparation, you too can join their ranks. So where do you start?

Job or college interviews

There are a few basic differences between college and job interviews. Colleges interview many people because they have several places on offer and have to allow for students deciding to accept a place elsewhere. This is not true of job interviews. Employers are usually filling only one vacancy and they will rarely interview more than about eight people. They may have already selected the eight from many, many application forms they have received. So once you have been offered a job interview, the odds in your favour have already narrowed impressively. In either case, if you are invited for interview, you must have convinced the interviewer, on paper at least, that you are a good candidate. Interviewers do not waste their time interviewing people who have no chance of success.

What the interviewer wants

In a nutshell the interviewer wants you to say enough about yourself for him or her (or them) to decide whether you are suitable for the job or college place. This sounds obvious, but in fact there is some research which shows that interviews are not at all reliable in predicting people's ability to do a job, or their success on a course. Nevertheless, there are very few organisations willing to take the chance of going ahead without one. Some colleges, of course, take this chance, but the odds are that you will have to face an interview – indeed several interviews – during the course of your student/working life.

College interviewers are looking for people with the necessary qualifications who can convince them that:

- ◆ they'll turn up to at least a few lectures (it's bad for the lecturers' egos if they don't!)
- ◆ they'll complete the course (drop out rates don't look good to prospective students)
- ◆ they'll pass (high failure rates don't look so hot either . . .)
- ◆ they really know the course details (so don't get it mixed up with the course at another college –

they're never quite the same, are they?)
➤ they are actually interested in the course
   (amazingly, some students fail to appear to be)

However, people interviewing for jobs are also looking for the necessary:

Skills   Knowledge   Personality

So you need to know what is expected of you in these areas and that means preparation.

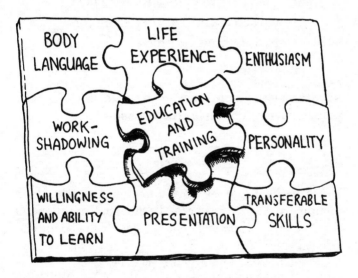

I have interviewed many people for both college places and jobs, and I estimate that only about 60 per cent of them had done some preparation. Not necessarily enough, but some. That leaves about 40 per cent who had done no preparation at all. Mary, for instance, a 19 year-old who was applying for a clerk/typist job got halfway through the interview and then asked 'What does your company actually do?' Well, would you have given her the job?

Preparation

By the time that you have found a job or college course you want to apply for, you will have already undertaken the following work. You will have, won't you?

- ➨ Researched the organisation or college (see page 26)
- ➨ Researched the job/course (see page 27)
- ➨ Prepared a CV, application form or both
- ➨ Undertaken an evaluation of your skills

 I like to see candidates who have worked as hard at preparing for the interview as I have. **"**

Quote from a personnel manager

Many people are unsure how to go about evaluating their skills, but it is quite simple once you know how.

Exercise

You have been out of work since leaving school six months ago. You haven't been idle though. You've done all the housework, shopping and cooking for the family and minded your little sister after school. What skills have you used? You can find my suggestions below.

You can do the same sort of exercise for anything you have been doing. For example:

- ➨ any kind of work you have done in the past (paper round, etc)
- ➨ voluntary work (including helping the neighbours)
- ➨ studying
- ➨ club or team membership or leadership

Exercise answers

You have been doing the shopping, housework and cooking for your family as well as looking after your little sister after school. Assuming you've been making a good job of it, here are some of the skills you will probably have used:

Budgeting for the shopping
Reliability collecting sister from school, having meals ready
Observation noticing the dirt and dealing with it
Patience dealing with sister
Organisation to get everything done
Prioritising deciding what to do when
Time management fitting everything into the time allowed, and still getting to the school gates
Motivation getting yourself going
Message-taking when people knock on the door or the phone rings
Honesty not stealing the milk money!

I'm sure you can think of others, but this will give you some ideas.

Continue analysing your skills in this way until you are confident that you have listed them all. Now you are ready to prepare yourself for your one big chance to convince the interviewer that you are the best thing since sliced bread ...

Skills, qualifications and knowledge are important, but they are not the complete answer. Interviewers are looking for other things, too.

Exercise

What the interviewer wants

Put yourself in the interviewer's position (usually the big superior chair!). Imagine you are about to interview someone for a job or a college place. You will be spending perhaps a whole day interviewing up to eight people. You've done a good job at the preparation stage. You have carefully considered all the application forms and are sure that all those people invited for interview have the necessary skills and qualifications. What, then, are you looking for?

Keeping in mind the interview you are preparing for, write a list of ten things you think the interviewer may be looking for. These should be general points and not skills or qualification specific. Keep your answers in your interview file. Look at them before each interview you attend to refresh your memory. Remember, the list may need changing for each interview.

Exercise answers

Here are some suggestions. You may have thought of other things.

1. Someone who will fit in with the existing work or student group.
2. Someone who is clean and reasonably tidy.
3. Someone who is likeable.
4. Someone who is not overqualified (or they may get bored and leave quickly).

5. Someone who is clear about what they want from the job and the organisation (or college and course).
6. Someone who is clear about what they can offer the organisation/course.
7. Someone who speaks well and gets points across clearly.
8. Someone who has thought about how they can use their existing skills and knowledge, even if they are not exactly the same as those required in the job or course on offer.
9. Someone who knows what they want in the future.
10. Someone who is flexible.

Martin John Yate in his book *Great Answers to Tough Interview Questions* (Kogan Page, 1988), takes this further. He lists a number of personal and professional qualities that employers look for. The good news is that you can have all these qualities without having had a single job.

Exercise

Look through Yate's list below and think about how you could show an interviewer that you had each quality. (For example, you could show them you had a lot of drive when you took an evening class to get an extra qualification.)

Personal qualities
  Drive knowing where you're going
  Motivation getting on without supervision, being willing to find out how to do things
  Communication skills this can include both the written and spoken word
  Chemistry the ability to get on with people
  Energy having plenty of get-up-and-go
  Determination someone with stamina, who sees a job through to the end

Confidence assertiveness, not looking down on anyone or being intimidated by seniors

Professional qualities
Reliability being dependable
Honesty/integrity essential; no one likes to work with people they can't trust. People will appreciate knowing where they are with you. It doesn't mean you have to be blunt, but you have to be assertive and honest in your dealings with others.
Pride taking pride in yourself and your work
Dedication putting that bit of extra effort into your work
Analytical skills an ability to step back and look at a problem from various angles
Listening skills really hearing what people are saying. Taking account of the difference between what is said and what is meant.

This list may seem daunting but there is one big thing to remember: interviewers want everyone who walks through the door to be able to do the job or succeed on the course. They want to have a hard time making a choice. This means that they are on your side. They are not out to trip you up, make you feel silly or show you how inadequate you are. They want you to be good.

Interviewers' score sheets – job and college applications

Another way to think about what interviewers want is to look at how they'll be 'marking' you. Colleges and business organisations are equally likely to use score sheets of one sort or another. Of course, I must emphasise that not all interviewers are this organised. They should make notes as they go along (so don't be put off if they do) and they should have some impartial way of recording what they think of you. This helps them to be objective about the applicants and to remember at the end of the day what they thought of each person.

There is no set way of doing this, but so that you have an idea of the sort of format your interviewer may be using here is one which is used by an organisation employing 3,000 people.

INTERVIEW ASSESSMENT FORM

Job Title

Candidate   **Interviewer(s)**

Rating Scale: **A** = Outstanding   **B** = Above average

C = Average   **D** = Below average

Characteristics Rating Notes

1	**Appearance & physical characteristics**	A	B	C	D
	Looks/Grooming				
	Dress				
	Voice/Speech				
	Eyesight				
	Disabilities				

2	**Educational qualifications**	A	B	C	D
	School				
	Higher				
	Professional/Job Training				

3	**Work-shadowing**	A	B	C	D
	Type(s) of work				
	Level of work				
	Duration				

4	**Intelligence and special aptitudes**	A	B	C	D
	General intelligence				
	Facility with written words				
	Facility with figures				

				A	B	C	D
Public-speaking							
Ability to drive	Yes/No Endorsements?						
Car owner?	Yes/No						
Special interest(s)							

5	**Social skills**	A	B	C	D
	Leadership/Managerial				
	Assertiveness				
	Colleague relationships				
	External contacts				
	Tact/Diplomacy				

6	**Motivation**	A	B	C	D
	Commitment to task				
	Self-reliance				
	Stress tolerance				
	Attitudes				
	Career ambitions				

7   Personal circumstances

Sex*

Age range

Marital Status*

Mobility

Summary

_____

_____

_____

_____

_____

_____

Signature of interviewer:

Date:

*Check implications of Sex Discrimination Act.

It is fairly obvious that the interviewer(s) will not be checking every item for every job, and before the interview they can simply cross off those items which don't apply. If there is more than one interviewer, this type of score sheet can make sure that they make their own judgments about candidates, rather than simply be swayed by another interviewer's ideas on the interviewee.

Having said that, research shows that there is little agreement between interviewers over the same candidate. There again, I have often interviewed with other people, and my experience would contradict the research because generally I have found that interviewers have quite similar views.

The truth, the whole truth and nothing but the truth?

During an interview you must always tell the truth. If you lie and are found out you could lose the job or place offer.

However, there are ways and ways of telling the truth. This is one of the well-recognised rules of the interviewing game.

For example, supposing you have three main hobbies – reading, seeing friends and music. The job you are going for requires you to be very sociable but you actually spend a fair bit of your time alone reading or playing music. You don't emphasise that. You talk about your other, quite genuine hobby – seeing friends.

I know of someone who applied for a job as head of department in a hospital. When asked if he had ever done similar work before, he answered 'Yes, at — hospital I managed the — department.' Sounds okay, doesn't it? He actually managed it for one afternoon whilst his boss was out of the office. He got the job! I wouldn't recommend that you go this far though – you may find yourself in trouble later.

So, tell the truth, but use the truth to highlight those strengths you possess that will help you succeed at the interview.

By the way, there are gender differences here. I hate to say it (and I'm generalising here), but men are much better at bluffing in interviews. Women are too honest. If a man and woman, each with the same limited experience of doing a certain task were asked if they had relevant experience, the man would probably say something like 'Yes, I have done that', whilst a woman would qualify it by saying something like 'Well, I've done it, but only once or twice.' Both answers are honest, but the second is unnecessarily and unhelpfully detailed. (Remember, the interviewer can ask for more details if they want them.) One of women's strengths is their ability to communicate honestly, but this is one occasion when they should take a leaf out of men's books, and disclose only limited information where appropriate.

If you have trouble with this, try to imagine a BIG pair of scissors cutting off your speech at the end of what you really need to say. Then close your mouth and wait for the next question!

Typical interview format

Whether you are attending a job or college interview, you can feel reasonably sure that the main body of the interview will follow a fairly predictable format. It will be along the lines of:

1 Welcome, sitting down, etc
2 Settling-in questions
3 Telling you about the organisation or college
4 Education questions
5 Experience questions
6 Your turn to ask questions
7 Interview finishes

Every part of the interview is equally important – the interviewer is trying to get a picture of you as a whole person. However, you can see that the key part of the interview is when the interviewer questions you and it is this section that we will concentrate on first. Your task will be to present your education and/or work experience so that they match what the interviewer is looking for.

Preparing for questions

The actual question and answer session is usually the part of the interview people feel least confident about handling well. The good news is that with preparation you can anticipate almost every question you're likely to be asked.

The type of questions asked will depend on a number of things:

- the style and experience of the interviewer
- whether the organisation has an equal opportunities policy
- the nature of the job, organisation, college or course
- the information you have provided in your application

Basically, we ask everyone the same questions, but add one or two extras depending on what's in their application form.

Quote from a college lecturer

Using your background material

Chapter seven will give you further details of what to expect from different types of interview. From a practical point of view, you should prepare for every question you can possibly think you might be asked no matter what type of interview you anticipate. So, how do you manage this? Well, you use the full range of information available to you, which should include:

- ➤ your application form, CV, Record of Achievement or GNVQ portfolio (see Chapter 6)
- ➤ information about the organisation or college
- ➤ information about the course from the prospectus
- ➤ *or* information about the job from the job description tion and, if available, the person specification
- ➤ your research into the organisation or college
- ➤ an analysis of your skills

Information about organisations and colleges can be found by:

- ➤ asking around, especially if the organisation is local
- ➤ reading local newspapers or national ones, if appropriate
- ➤ asking the library what information they have – companies have to keep financial records and these and other information may well be available at your library. There is a list of suitable sources of information at the back of this book.

- ➤ knowing about current issues in the area of your choice (eg if you are applying to medical school, consider the changes in the structure of the NHS – the interviewer will expect you to have at least some knowledge of them)
- ➤ trade/professional magazines or journals

If you are applying for a college place you will have a fair idea about the course you have applied for. You should also have (or have found out) some information about the college and its locality.

If you are applying for a job you should have received from the organisation a job description, a person specification and information about the organisation.

A job description describes the *job to be done*. It may also give you additional information such as salary scale and who the postholder is responsible to.

A person specification describes the *type of person who can do the job*. Often you will see a letter (usually E or D) beside each item. The purpose of this is to identify whether that skill or personal quality is essential (E) or desirable (D).

Information about the organisation can vary from nothing at all to a very detailed information pack.

However, there is no guarantee that you will be sent all or indeed any of these documents. So what can you do if you are not? You could phone the person responsible for the vacancy and ask for further details. Better still, if the place you're applying to isn't too far away, call in to collect the information. It will give you an opportunity to look round and see how long the journey takes. If you have a job description you could sit and work out what you think the person specification would include. Simply ask yourself 'What personal, professional or educational qualities would a person doing this type of work need to have?' Alternatively, you may have to rely on your own research into the organisation.

To make the most effective use of all these documents you should go through them underlining those words which appear to be most important. Once you have done this, it is not difficult to work out the sort of questions you might be asked.

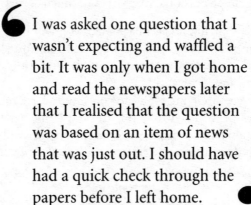

I was asked one question that I wasn't expecting and waffled a bit. It was only when I got home and read the newspapers later that I realised that the question was based on an item of news that was just out. I should have had a quick check through the papers before I left home.

Quote from someone who had just been for an interview as a researcher with the Department of Social Security

Here are a sample job description and person specification for a sales assistant's position in a fashion shop. Significant words have been underlined.

Job Description

Job Title: .... Shop Assistant ....

Responsible to: .... Store Manager ....

Duties

1. To ensure that the shop is <u>tidy</u> before opening time each morning

2. To <u>assist customers</u> with requests about merchandise

3. To <u>staff the tills</u> as necessary

4. To <u>staff the changing room</u> as necessary

5. To keep the shop and merchandise <u>tidy</u> at all times

6. To <u>answer the telephone</u>

Person Specification

This person specification lists the criteria necessary for the person we seek to appoint.

a   <u>Fashionably dressed</u> in a way appropriate to the nature of the store
b.   <u>Clean and tidy</u>
c.   Able to <u>work unsupervised</u>
d.   Able to <u>think ahead</u> and make decisions
e.   Experience at <u>staffing tills</u>
f.   Experience at <u>answering the telephone</u>
g.   Willingness to <u>work as part of a team</u>
h.   <u>Non-smoker</u> or willing not to smoke during working hours
i.   <u>Experience at selling</u>
j.   <u>Experience at handling customers</u>

Items (a), (b), (g), and (h) are essential. Other items are desirable.

Exercise

Below are a job description and person specification for a clerk/typist vacancy with a company that provides training courses. Look at these documents and highlight or underline those words which you consider to be important clues to what you will be expected to be able to do, or qualities the interviewer will be looking for.

Job Description

Job Title: ....Clerk/Typist...
Post No: ....234...
Scale: ....A/B...
Responsible to: .....Office.Manager..................................

Main purpose of job

To support the office manager and her secretary in the day-to-day running of the training section.

Specific duties

1.   To undertake typing for the office manager as instructed by the senior secretary
2.   To keep the office filing up to date
3.   To act as relief receptionist during holiday periods
4.   To keep the training library tidy and ensure that all resource material is checked out and returned on time
5.   To proof-read newly developed course material
6.   To book venues and catering for courses

Person Specification

Job title: Clerk/Typist

The following person specification lists the criteria applicable to the person we seek to recruit for the above post.

a.	Ability to type at least 35 wpm	E
b.	Good attention to detail	E
c.	Telephone answering skills	D
d.	Good organisational skills	E
e.	Ability to work unsupervised	D
f.	Knowledge of training business	D
g.	Knowledge of word-processing	D
h.	Knowledge of desk top publishing	D
i.	GCSE English language	E
j.	Non-smoker	E

D   Desirable criteria   E   Essential criteria

Exercise answers

You should have underlined the following words in the job description and person specification.

Job Description

Job Title: Clerk/Typist

Post No: ....234..

Scale: ....A/B..

Responsible to: ...Office Manager...................................

Main purpose of job

To support the office manager and her secretary in the day-to-day running of the training section.

Specific duties

1. To undertake <u>typing</u> for the office manager as instructed by the senior secretary

2. To keep the office <u>filing</u> up to date

3. To act as <u>relief receptionist</u> during holiday periods

4. To keep the training library <u>tidy</u> and ensure that all resource material is checked out and returned <u>on time</u>

5. To <u>proof-read</u> newly developed course material

6. To <u>book venues and catering</u> for courses.

Person Specification

Job title: ..Clerk/Typist...

The following person specification lists the criteria applicable to the person we seek to recruit for the above post.

a.	Ability to <u>type at least 35 wpm</u>	E
b.	Good <u>attention to detail</u>	E
c.	<u>Telephone answering skills</u>	D
d.	Good <u>organisational skills</u>	E
e.	Ability to <u>work unsupervised</u>	D
f.	<u>Knowledge of training business</u>	D
g.	Knowledge of <u>word-processing</u>	D
h.	Knowledge of <u>desk top publishing</u>	D
i.	<u>GCSE English language</u>	E
j.	<u>Non-smoker</u>	E

D   Desirable criteria   E   Essential criteria

Taking the items one at a time, it is clear the interviewer will ask questions about:

Skills typing, filing, telephone, organisation, general office skills

Education to ensure that you have a reasonable standard of English

Knowledge of the training business (you should have looked this up if you didn't have any idea beforehand)

Attitudes ability to work unsupervised, to be polite to customers, willingness to train, etc

In fact, this is the type of exercise you should have undertaken before you completed the application form or amended your CV when applying for the job. If you did, you're streets ahead.

In doing this you will see where your own skills, qualifications and experience match with the information provided. Don't worry if there is not an exact match. Early in your career, it is unlikely that you will have had an opportunity to gain a wide range of experience. Employers will be looking to see whether you have any *transferable* skills or experience. That is, experience in similar areas which suggest an appropriate aptitude. You will also need to consider transferable skills and knowledge if you are applying for a college place that is not directly linked to your GCSEs, A-levels or Highers. Armed with all this information, you can begin to work out the questions you are likely to be asked and how you might answer them. This is covered in much more detail in the next two chapters, but the following exercise will give you a start.

Exercise

Imagine you are going to interview someone for the clerk/typist job we've looked at. Using the job description and person specification provided, write down as many interview questions as you can think of.

Exercise answers

Some questions which might be asked at this interview for a clerk/typist are:

1. What experience do you have which is relevant to this post?
2. How fast can you type?
3. What word-processing packages are you familar with?
4. Give me an example of your organisational skills.
5. How do you manage your time?
6. What qualities do you think are important in a receptionist?
7. How would you organise booking venues for courses?
8. What do you know about business training?
9. Do you know how to use a desk top publishing system?
10. Give me an example of your attention to fine detail.
11. How do you think you will manage if you have to work unsupervised?
12. How do you make decisions?

When you are applying for any college place or job, this is the process you should go through.

Questions

You should keep in mind with all questions:

- ▸ what the interviewer has told you during the introductory talk usually given at the beginning of the interview. Listen hard to this, it may give you valuable clues on how to 'shape' your answers.
- ▸ what the interviewer is trying to find out
- ▸ think about what the interviewer fears – for example, is a question about your ability to study masking a fear that you might drop out? Does a

question about your typing speeds reflect a fear that the work won't get done? Work out the fear and you may have a clearer idea of how to phrase your answer.

- how you can best show that you can do the job/complete the course
- how you can minimise your weaknesses
- how you can highlight your strengths
- the need to sound positive and enthusiastic. No one wants to work with or teach someone who's miserable or boring. Don't overdo it, but try to throw in the odd positive word like 'enjoy', 'enthusiastic', etc.
- never criticise others in your answers. The interviewer may think that you will be a troublemaker.
- try to always give an example to back up your answers
- interviewers will know the answers to some of the questions they ask because they should have studied your application material. However, you should answer the questions as if they know nothing about you. You might occasionally, though, like to say something like 'Well, as you know . . .'
- give yourself time to answer. Think before you speak.

> I reckon less than 25 per cent of 16 year-olds I see prepare for the interview. Sometimes when I ask them why they want to do this (continuous assessment) course they say "because I don't cope well with the pressure of exams". Hopeless!

Quote from a BTEC lecturer

Questioning techniques

Interviewers are taught different types of general questions, which they can use in all situations. These are called:

1 closed questions

2 leading questions

3 multiple questions

4 probing questions

5 open questions

6 hypothetical questions

The skilled interviewer will be well aware of how to use these questions, and the different responses to expect from each one. Do remember, though, that not all interviewers are skilled!

1 Closed questions

These are questions that can easily be answered with a simple 'yes' or 'no'.

> 'So, you've been living in Bradford for three years?'
> 'You'll be 19 next month then?'
> 'You passed, what, three GCSEs?'

These questions are useful for finding out or clarifying information. But beware. Some interviewers are not skilled and will ask you a closed question when they actually want a longer answer. Do not be afraid to elaborate a little. For example, for the first question above you might answer:

> 'Yes, I like it here very much and have no plans to move.'

This will tell the interviewer that you're not going to vanish to another location once you've gained experience and training from the organisation.

It drives me crazy when people answer a question with simply "yes" or "no", even if I have been silly enough to ask a closed question. Why should I have to do all the work to drag the information out of them?

Quote from a director of a printing company

2 Leading questions

These questions strongly suggest how they should be answered.

> 'You shouldn't find this type of course too difficult then, should you?'
> 'Well, I suppose you're expecting to earn between £ — and £ — ?'

This is a poor questioning technique and one which interviewers should avoid because the canny interviewee will quickly reply in the expected manner. Having said that, I've found they still manage to do it! I was actually told the maximum the company was prepared to pay me by a personnel manager once. I replied 'That'll do nicely!'

3 Multiple questions

Multiple questions are a sign of a poorly trained interviewer, because they are so difficult to answer. Multiple questions are simply when the interviewer asks several questions at once.

> 'So, what did you enjoy at college? Was it exciting being away from home for the first time? And what did that teach you that you can use here?'

If you are unlucky enough to be faced with this type of questioning, keep calm. Remember as many of the questions as you can and then say:

'Well, if I could answer your first question first . . .'

and so on until you've answered them all. You may have to ask the interviewer to repeat them, although the odds are that they won't remember them either!

START MADE APPLICATION	OFFERED INTERVIEW — FORWARD 2	LOOKED GOOD — FORWARD 1	PREPARED WELL — FORWARD 3
FINISH YOUR PRIZE: EXCEL AT INTERVIEW! GREAT PARTING LINE — FORWARD 1	? THE ? INTERVIEW ? GAME ?		4 UNEXPECTED QUESTIONS — BACK 4 ANSWERED EXPERIENCE QUESTIONS WELL — FORWARD 1
DIDN'T ESTABLISH RAPPORT WITH ALL INTERVIEWERS — BACK 2	GOOD LIST OF QUESTIONS FOR INTERVIEWER — FORWARD 1	GOOD PERSONAL QUESTIONS — FORWARD 2	DIDN'T PUSH BEST POINTS — BACK 2

4 Probing questions
Probing questions delve a little further into whatever is being discussed.

'Can you tell me a little more about that . . . ?'
'What happened then?'

Skilled interviewers are likely to use this technique to encourage you to expand your answers.

5 Open questions
These are the questions used most commonly by an experienced interviewer. They are questions which are difficult to answer with 'yes' or 'no'.

Open questions often begin with:

- who
- when
- why
- what
- how
- where

'How do you see your career developing?'
'What have you learnt most from your A-level study?'
'What do you think you will find most difficult about this course?'

Many interviewers recognise that open questions are also a way of encouraging nervous or quiet people to speak.

So, when you are considering what type of questions you might be asked, word them as open questions, because this is the sort you are most likely to meet.

6 Hypothetical questions

This is when the interviewer poses a problem and asks you how you would handle it. They are usually questions relating to the job or course you're applying for, but be prepared. I have heard college lecturers ask questions like 'If you were prime minister what would you do about . . .' An example of a job-related question would be:

'You have four urgent pieces of work on your desk, and only time to finish two of them. How would you decide which two?'

If you can't answer this from direct experience or intelligent guesswork, the trick is to refer back to a similar situation you have known. Simply say 'Well, I had a situation a bit like that in . . . Could I tell you how I dealt with that?' This is perfectly acceptable as the interviewer is trying to find out about your skills or a particular aspect of your personality rather than how you would deal with that one particular situation.

Chapter Checklist

Do you feel you know:

- ❏ what the interviewer is looking for?

- ❏ what the interviewer fears?

- ❏ how organised interviewers 'score' candidates?

- ❏ what to expect from a typical interview format?

- ❏ how to answer questions when you want to be selective with the truth?

- ❏ how to use background material?

- ❏ how to use job descriptions, person specifications or course details to help you plan for the interview?

- ❏ how to cope with different questioning techniques?

  - ➡ open
  - ➡ leading
  - ➡ multiple
  - ➡ closed
  - ➡ probing
  - ➡ hypothetical

- ❏ how to work out for yourself what type of questions you may be asked at your interview?

2 Questions and Answers for Job and College Interviews

You should read this chapter:

➡ as soon as you begin to apply for jobs or college places
➡ when preparing for a specific interview

By the end of this chapter you should know:

➡ how to use the first few questions to help you feel comfortable during the interview
➡ how to answer settling-in questions
➡ how to answer questions about your education and qualifications
➡ how to answer questions about your skills and experience
➡ how to answer questions about yourself as a person
➡ how to answer questions about your leisure interests

The answers given throughout this chapter are only suggestions. There isn't ever one right answer and your own situation will determine what you say.

Settling-in questions

The interviewer is likely to begin the interview with some very easy-to-answer questions. This is done so that you can relax and get your brain in gear. If the interviewer collects you from the waiting area, you may be asked the first question as you walk to the interview room. These questions are likely to be something like:

Q 'How was your journey?' or 'Did you find us okay?'

What is the interviewer looking for?
The interviewer is just settling you in. Okay, so you got on

the wrong bus, and got chased by a rabid Rottweiler. You don't say so. You say something like:

A 'Fine. I was surprised at how quickly I got here. The buses are quite convenient.'

Why?
This is a tiny plus point from a starter question. It lets the interviewer know that you are capable of finding your way round (especially important if you are applying for college places away from home). Don't worry too much about selling yourself with this type of settling-in question though, there's plenty of opportunity for that later.

 'Tell me about yourself.'

What is the interviewer looking for?
The interviewer wants to know about you in relation to the job or college place. If you're applying for a job, your answer might include information about the stability of your home life, if that's relevant – to show that you'll stay in the job after the company has spent time and money training you. But, this is not the time to tell the interviewer you've got a cat named Toto and your little brother is a pain in the neck.

Tell the truth, but be selective, remembering that the interviewer is most interested in you in relation to the job, or course.

Supposing you left school 18 months ago and have been working in a bookshop. You're now applying for a job as a bank clerk. Look back at your research. What were the essential details mentioned in the information you received? What skills, knowledge and experience do you have that are relevant? You may answer with something like:

A 'Well, I'm 18 and I've lived in this area all my life and come from a close family. I enjoyed school and did well with my exams. When I was looking at careers options, I realised that I enjoyed being with people as well as reading, so I took a job in a bookshop to combine the two interests. But now I've realised that I'd like a job that offers more challenge and has more career prospects. My family have been with this bank for years and it has a good reputation. That's why I've applied for this job now.'

Why?
This answer gives an overview of relevant information about yourself in relation to the job.

Alternatively, if you are asked this question at the beginning of a college interview, you might reply along the lines of:

'Well, I'm 18 and have lived in this city all my life. I have a sister and two brothers who all live locally. I became interested in drama during my first year at my present school. My older sister had a lead part in the school play and I used to hang around and watch what was going on. Since then I've really developed this interest. As you'll see from my application form, I'm taking English and drama at Higher level and I'm a very active member of the local amateur dramatics society.'

Why?
Again, this tells the interviewer a bit about you, and highlights your enthusiasm and the fact that your liking for your subject is not a passing whim.

 'Do you feel confident that you know all about the job/course you're applying for?' or 'Have you had a chance to study the job description/course details?'

What is the interviewer looking for?
This question may follow on from the interviewer telling

you about the job or course at the beginning of the interview. Alternatively, it may be a warming-up question. Let's assume that you do have a pretty good idea of what's involved, but however good job descriptions or course details are, you will probably think of some area where you are not clear. You may have something to ask from your list of questions prepared for the end of the interview.

A 'Well, I got a lot of information about the job/course from the information you sent me, and I'm really interested in — . One thing I'm not clear about though, is what proportion of time is spent on each task/subject?'

Why?
This shows that you've really studied the job description or course outline and are interested in greater detail. It might give you an opportunity to sell yourself further. For example, if the interviewer tells you that about 20 per cent of the time is spent speaking to customers on the phone, you may be able to reply that you enjoy telephone work. If you are told that 25 per cent of the course is spent on a particular topic you can demonstrate that you know something about it, or at least that you are enthusiastic to learn.

> Well, I keep in mind whether the person sitting in front of me during the interview is boring. After all, if I'm going to be sitting in seminars with them for several years, that can be important.

Quote from a college lecturer

Exercise

Imagine that you have just been invited to tell a prospective interviewer about yourself. Keep in mind the job or course you are applying for. What would you say? Make some notes and keep them in your interview file.

Education questions

Whilst questions about your education may not feature much in interviews as you get older, they are likely to be quite important at this stage of your life, whether you are applying for a job or a college place. Typical education questions are:

1. When did you leave school?
2. What school did you attend?
3. What qualifications did you get?
4. What was your favourite subject at school?
5. What subject did you dislike most?
6. Did you play sports?
7. What do you think school/college really taught you?

8. What did you enjoy most about school or college?
9. What did you like least about school or college?
10. Who was your favourite teacher? Why?
11. Did you belong to any clubs?
12. What work-shadowing did you undertake? What did you learn from it?
13. Why did/didn't you go on to further education?
14. Would you like to continue your education in any way? How?
15. Did you take any extra responsibility at school, such as being a prefect?
16. What did you do in your year off?

Let's look at some questions in detail, then you can try to answer some for yourself.

Q 'Why didn't you go on to further education?'

What is the interviewer looking for?
Simply to know your motives for ending your full-time education at this stage.

A Remember to tell the truth, but express it to your benefit. You might say something like:
'Well, I'd got as far as I wanted to go with formal education, and I feel I'd rather take courses related to the career I want to follow. I enjoy studying though, and I know that this company has a good reputation for offering training to staff. I'd like to develop some professional abilities that way.'

Why?
This tells the interviewer a number of things about you. You don't think you know it all and you're willing to give up some of your time to study. Also, by saying 'I know your company...', you sound positive, as if you expect to be working for them.

Q 'Who was your favourite teacher? Why?'

What is the interviewer looking for?
Your answer will say something about the sort of person you are as well as the sort of person the teacher is.

A 'Ms LaRouche our science teacher. She gave such lively lectures and gave us a lot of help with our assignments.'

Why?
This may be fine, it shows an interest in the subject. (You will make sure you choose a relevant example, won't you?) But if you are applying for a job or college place where you will have to work largely unsupervised, you might want to add that you can, of course, work alone. Be truthful, but select which of the teacher's qualities you choose to highlight.

Q 'Why do you want to do this particular course?'

What is the interviewer looking for?
The interviewer wants to know:

- ➡ that you really know about the course, the subjects it covers, etc. So prepare well.
- ➡ that you have thought how the course fits in with the studying you have done in the past
- ➡ any future career ideas you have

A 'Well, as you will see from my application form, I did sociology A-level and that's my real interest. I want to live and study in this region, so I've compared all the available sociology courses. I see that this one has a strong research element and, as I'm thinking about a career in social research, this course seems to offer what I'm looking for.'

Why?
You have displayed all the qualities listed above. In addition, you have shown that you have compared courses and made a considered choice. Also, you have looked at the location and would actively choose to live there.

Q 'I see you are taking three A-levels. How many hours a week do you study at home?'

What is the interviewer looking for?
The interviewer wants to know:

- ➡ that you are prepared to put in the time necessary to pass your courses
- ➡ whether you are struggling just to keep up at your current course level. If this is the case, it might indicate that you wouldn't be able to keep up with a more demanding course.

A 'I study each evening for an hour and a half, and for about five hours over the weekend. I also use my free periods at college to work. I think that having a social life is important, so I have Friday evenings off and go out sometime over the weekend. I think it's vital to plan ahead, but to be flexible if need be.'

Why?
This shows that you are able to plan ahead, manage your time effectively and yet still have a social life. It also demonstrates that you are that desirable creature: a well-rounded person.

Q 'I see you're doing one GNVQ and one A-level. What do you think that doing the GNVQ course has given you that another A-level wouldn't have?'

What is the interviewer looking for?
Because GNVQ is a new qualification, it is quite possible

that your interviewer will not know very much about it. He or she will be interested in the differences between the two qualifications in terms of i) learning/teaching style, and ii) what those differences have meant to YOU.

A 'The GNVQ course involves lots of project work – it's much more practical, and less about how much you can remember for an exam than an A-level. I know that the project work has made me more self-confident, because I have to find things out for myself, and work out my own ways of tackling problems. Doing the GNVQ has also made me pretty organised – there's a lot to get through.

'The other thing I really enjoy about the GNVQ is the nuts and bolts aspect – you're dealing with real businesses (people/designs/etc) rather than abstract theories. The work experience has been a real eye-opener, and persuaded me that I want to work in . . .

'I'm glad I took the A-level too, though. Doing the essays definitely developed my written skills, and that helped with the project write-ups for the GNVQ.'

Why?
You have said positive things about both qualifications. You have explained that the GNVQ course has a different style from the A-level by mentioning the:

- project work
- work experience
- down-to-earth approach

You have highlighted some qualities you have gained from that:

- self-confidence
- good organisational skills

➜➜ you can find things out and solve problems for yourself

Finally, you've shown you are enthusiastic about tackling a real, practical job (although of course you wouldn't emphasise this if it's a college place you are applying for).

> We always get a reference from the head teacher and we really take notice of what they say. For example, if a student did less well in an exam because of teacher illness, we take that into account.

Quote from a college interviewer

Exercise

Make some notes on your answers to the questions below. Remember, if you go for more than one interview, you will probably need to review these answers to fit in with various job/college requirements. Keep your completed sheets in your interview file.

What work-shadowing did you do at school? What did you learn from it?

➜➜ What is the interviewer looking for?
➜➜ How will you answer the question?
➜➜ What strengths have you highlighted?

What was your favourite subject at school/college? Why?

➜➜ What is the interviewer looking for?
➜➜ How will you answer the question?
➜➜ What strengths have you highlighted?

Personal questions

Almost every interviewer who knows what they're doing will ask you personal questions. These are not of the 'How many girlfriends have you had?' variety, but are personal inasmuch as the answers you give demonstrate the sort of person you are as opposed to giving information about your skills and education. These questions can often be the most tricky because the interviewer's aim is to get you to reflect on yourself as a whole person. Common personal questions are:

1. Why do you want to do this course/job?
2. Why should we give you a place/offer you the job?
3. What are your strengths/weaknesses?
4. Where do you see yourself in five/ten years' time?
5. What would your friends say that they like/find irritating about you?
6. How did you get on with your boss/teacher?
7. Why do you want to come here?
8. What have you achieved in life so far?
9. What is your health like?
10. What do you think your references will say?
11. Which decisions are difficult for you to make?
12. What do you think you can offer this organisation/college?
13. Tell me about something you have done which you are proud of.
14. What do you think is the most important thing about being a…?
15. What did you find most difficult at…?

They all need a bit of thinking about, don't they? Let's look at a couple of the more common ones.

Q 'If people were talking about you, what weaknesses would they feel you have?'

What is the interviewer looking for?
Actually, the interviewer is trying to get you to think about what weaknesses *you* think you have, so don't spend ages thinking about every criticism that's ever been heaped on you.

A 'It's hard to know how others see you, but I suppose one weakness I'm aware of is that I can feel very enthusiastic about starting something and then get bored when it's underway. I've worked out how to overcome that, though, by careful planning and by giving myself deadlines.'

Why?
Always answer this type of question by a) stating the weakness and b) explaining how you've overcome it. Okay, so you can't spell, are moody and hopelessly disorganised. Don't say so! NEVER tell the interviewer about a weakness which you still need to work on. ALWAYS tell them about one you've cracked. You're not telling a lie, you're just choosing which bit of the truth to tell. They can always ask you for more information.

Q 'What do you think your references will say about you?'

What is the interviewer looking for?
This is very similar to the question above, but gives you an opportunity to talk about your strengths as well as/instead of your weaknesses. Be realistic when you select what to say, because the interviewer may actually compare your answer with the references! It's very strange, but most people would much rather tell you their failings than their good points. But this is no time for false modesty. If you're good at something why shouldn't you say so? Don't be afraid to sell yourself, this is a very good opportunity for you to do so.

A 'I know that Mrs Jones was very pleased with my

exam results and I imagine she would comment on that. Also, I'm very organised and like to plan ahead – I always get my work done in good time. She might say too, that although I can work alone I do like to be with other people. I was part of the debating society at school and enjoy team sports.'

Why?
With this answer you've highlighted:

- ➤ an awareness of what one teacher thinks of an aspect of your ability
- ➤ your self- and time-management skills
- ➤ your ability to get along with other people
- ➤ the fact that you like to be part of a team
- ➤ your ability to work alone

Five strong points in one short answer. Not bad!

> ❝ I asked one man the usual question "Why should I give you this job rather than one of the other candidates?" He replied "Because I've applied for 108 jobs and this is the first interview I've had." Sad. Needless to say he didn't get the job. ❞
>
> *Quote from an office manager*

Q 'Why should we offer you a place on this course/give you this job?'

What is the interviewer looking for?
The interviewer wants to know that you have some

knowledge of the organisation or college. THIS IS IMPORTANT – so find out. You need to show that you have considered both what the organisation or course can do for you and what you can offer in return.

A 'Well, as you can see from my examination results, I've been interested in science for several years now. As part of my Highers, I had to do a project on environmental issues and I became very interested in this area, in fact I got a grade 'A' for the project. I realised that I would like to have a career in this area so I looked through all the course prospectuses and yours looks to be exactly what I want. I'm hard-working and would see the course through and I'm really keen to get a good degree because I think I might want to do research in future.'

Why?
You have told the interviewer:

- you did well throughout your A-level course, not just in the exam
- you have chosen that college, not just taken pot luck
- you are prepared to work hard
- you are ambitious and are looking ahead

Many of the personal questions focus on your understanding of yourself, so you need to analyse yourself as thoroughly as you can prior to the interview. Ask friends and relations how they see you too – you might get some surprises!

Q 'What do you think you would find most difficult about being a . . . ?'

What is the interviewer looking for?
A real understanding of the job or course in question. Whilst the question asks about you, this might be a good

time to bring in any topical issues that have been in the press or trade or professional journals.

Let's assume the question was 'What do you think you would find most difficult about being a social worker?'

A 'I think that social work is difficult and demanding. You have to keep up to date with the legal side of things. I don't think I'd have any trouble with that because I enjoy that type of study. Probably I'd have most difficulty working with people who abuse their children. I don't suppose anybody likes that much. But it's an important part of the job and if you can get the family back together again, with everyone happy, it would be very rewarding.'

Why?
You've told the interviewer:

- ➪ you understand that there are legal constraints on how the job is done
- ➪ you are not unrealistic about working with difficult people, but think you can handle it and perhaps even find some job satisfaction.

By the way, social work lecturers hate being told 'I want to be a social worker because I want to help people.'

Exercise

Answer the questions below and keep your answers safely in your interview file.

1. Make notes of your weaknesses.
2. Now note how you have overcome each of these weaknesses.
3. Make notes about your strengths.
4. Make notes about why you have chosen a particular course/job.
5. Make notes about why you should be given a place or offered the job.

I always look at their interests
section first. This is a very practical
job. If they say they do DIY or
something else practical, I feel
more ready to believe that they
will be able to cope.

*Quote from a manager interviewing for a lab
technician's job*

Leisure questions

Some interviewers will consider leisure activities
important whilst others will ignore them. In your
interview preparation, however, you must assume they
will study them carefully.

Below are some typical leisure questions.

1.   What leisure activities do you enjoy?
2.   I see you're a member of . . . Tell me about it.
3.   All your leisure activities are very sociable. This job
     involves a lot of working alone. How will you cope?
4.   What do you get out of . . . ?
5.   What is there about your leisure activities that would
     help you in this job/college place?
6.   Would you describe yourself as sociable?

Let's look at an example.

 'What leisure activities do you enjoy?'

What is the interviewer looking for?
If this is a college interview, the interviewer may be
checking that you have not had to spend every minute
studying to get the grades you want. This means you
shouldn't answer that you don't have time for outside
activities because you are working so hard.

It may be that you do study hard, except on Fridays and Saturdays when you go out with friends. You may not consider that hanging around with friends constitutes a leisure activity, but re-worded it can sound just fine.

If you are asked this in a job interview, the interviewer may be checking:

- that you show some activities that match what you say on the rest of your application form
- the type of person you are to see if you would fit in with the existing work group

A 'I enjoy several different activities. I like to read – all sorts of books, but particularly thrillers. And I always try to get a part in the school play because I really like acting, although I'm also happy to do behind the scenes stuff. Also, I like socialising: I go out a couple of nights a week with friends.'

Why?

When you give this type of answer, you should provide information about yourself which is in keeping with that in earlier questions and answers. In this case:

➡ you've demonstrated that you enjoy at least one solitary activity (reading)

➡ you've shown that you like to be part of a team (acting), but

➡ you don't mind doing less glamorous work to ensure that the task gets done

➡ you're sociable

If you really do have very few leisure activities, are there any you could take up in advance of your interview? It is now that you will appreciate why your teachers have always told you to join something!

Skills and experience questions

These questions are more likely to be relevant if you are applying for a job, although you may well be asked them if you are applying for some sort of vocational training.

Typical skills and experience questions might be:

1. What experience do you have at . . . ?
2. If you were faced with this situation, how would you handle it?
3. What skills do you have at . . . ?
4. How fast can you . . . ?
5. How would you . . . ?
6. What equipment are you familiar with?
7. Have you ever used a . . . ?
8. How long have you . . . ?
9. When would you . . . ?
10. What are the main tasks of a . . . ?

Let's look at some in more detail.

Q 'What experience do you have at mending cars?'

What is the interviewer looking for?
The interviewer is trying to check your skills.

A 'Well, I got interested in cars when I used to help my mum fix our old banger. Then I discovered that our local youth club had a car mechanics course so I joined that. I learned a lot from them. We actually stripped an engine and put it back together. I enjoy this kind of work.'

Why?

This type of answer provides information about you and about your experience. It shows that:

- ◆→ you get on well with your mother, which they may think important if the job/course involves working with older people
- ◆→ you had the initiative to join a mechanics course
- ◆→ you're a positive person – 'enjoyed'
- ◆→ you seem to genuinely like this type of work

Q 'If you were asked to write/organise a major project how would you go about it?'

What is the interviewer looking for?

The interviewer might ask this general question or might specify a piece of work relevant to your studies or work. Either way, they are trying to find out how you organise yourself and your time. People who avoid undertaking a major project until the last minute put themselves under a lot of stress, which may affect other areas of their lives. In joint-study projects or working situations, this can sometimes affect how others work too.

A 'Well, it would depend on what the project was. I like to be organised and to break big tasks down into smaller sections so that I can give myself a series of deadlines. That way everything becomes more manageable. If it were appropriate, I would also try to consult or work with other people, too. I like being part of a team, and teams often achieve better results than an individual can.'

Why?
An answer like this gives a lot of information to a question that could be asked at either a job or college interview. You've told the interviewer that:

- you're a good time manager
- you're organised
- you're a good team player
- you appreciate that others have contributions to make
- you're self-motivated

Q 'What would you do if you were faced with . . . situation?'

What is the interviewer looking for?
This is a hypothetical question. Whilst the interviewer may well be looking for specific knowledge or skills, if it's clear that you don't yet have the relevant experience, try to convey:

- an ability to put past experience of a similar if not identical nature to good use
- an ability to think on your feet
- common sense
- the ability to keep calm

A Your answer will depend on the situation put to you. Remember the advice a few pages back: if you have no relevant experience DON'T PANIC. Just say to the interviewer 'I haven't had to handle that precise situation, but perhaps I could tell you about a time when . . .'

Why?
By answering this way, you have checked out with the interviewer that she or he is happy for you to use previous experience to answer this question. This type of answer is perfectly acceptable to most interviewers who are, after

all, trying to see how you work generally rather than in just one specific situation. It also shows that you can make connections between the tasks. It's worth repeating that you need to consider your transferable skills and experience, that is, how skills gained in one situation are useful in another context, eg dealing with an awkward person, working under pressure.

Exercise

Try to think of a typical situation you might be faced with on a course or job you're considering. How would you answer a question about your ability to deal with that situation so that you can demonstrate your strengths and some transferable skills.

1.   Give your answer to the question: How would you handle . . . ?
2.   List which of your strengths you have been able to highlight.
3.   List some transferable skills your answer implies you possess.

Remember, preparation is all. Try to work out every question you could be asked and how you would answer each one. Relate your answers not only to yourself and what you have to offer but also to the course outline or job description.

There is no need to learn answers off by heart. If you've thought through likely questions and answers beforehand, you'll be able to remember the points you want to make. This'll also help you to avoid sounding over-rehearsed, although this is usually not difficult because the same question can be asked in a number of different ways.

Chapter Checklist

❑ **Do you remember the settling-in questions you might be asked?**
- ➼ how was your journey?
- ➼ did you find us okay?
- ➼ how did you hear about this job/college?
- ➼ have you seen round the building?

❑ **Do you feel confident about answering questions about your education?**
- ➼ why you chose particular courses?
- ➼ why you left education after GCSEs?
- ➼ why you chose this course or job after your previous courses?

❑ **Have you analysed:**
- ➼ skills gained through work-shadowing, paid employment, and life experience?
- ➼ how your education will help you with whatever you are applying to do?
- ➼ how to present your experience in the most favourable light?

❑ **Have you decided how to demonstrate that:**
- ➼ your analysis of yourself is accurate and positive?
- ➼ you have the strengths to do the course or job?
- ➼ you have no major weaknesses (whilst still being truthful)?
- ➼ you are a self-motivated and enthusiastic person?

3 Awkward Questions

You should read this chapter:

➜ as soon as you begin to apply for jobs or college places

By the end of this chapter you should know:

➜ how to answer difficult questions about areas you would rather avoid
➜ the types of questions to ask at the end of the interview

Questions you don't want to be asked

I have talked in this book about always looking at your strong points and thinking positively. Now it's cringe time. I want you to think of all those questions you really, seriously, don't want to be asked. For example:

1. why you got sacked from your last job
2. why you had 20 spelling mistakes on your application form when you're applying for a job as a proof-reader
3. why you got such poor grades
4. why you show nothing in your 'Interests' section
5. why you're applying for this arts course when all your Highers are in science subjects
6. why you didn't finish that course
7. why your form shows a year missing

Now is the time to get out from behind the sofa and think about how you can turn these negative questions into positive answers. Remember, a good salesperson always sees an objection as an opportunity!

Q 'I see that you were a member of a heavy metal band for a year. What use do you think that might be to this organisation?'

What does the interviewer want to know?
Let's assume the interviewer isn't being sarcastic and really does want to know. Actually, even if you can detect sarcasm, you should answer this type of question seriously: never be trapped into displaying poor behaviour. We can learn something from almost every experience in life, even those that don't seem directly relevant.

A 'Yes, that was a good year which I really enjoyed, even though it was very hard work. I learned a lot from it. The band had to really pull together as a team to get through a long list of gigs and always give a good performance to the audience. I learned to keep calm when everyone around me was rushing around. Oh yes, and I learned to keep my temper when I was really tired and under pressure.'

Why?
You've shown the interviewer that:

- ➡➡ you can work as part of a team
- ➡➡ you are responsible and consider other people
- ➡➡ you are reliable
- ➡➡ you don't panic easily
- ➡➡ you work hard

All very desirable qualities to any employer or college.

Q 'Why were you sacked from your last job?'

What does the interviewer want to know?
Basically, what's wrong with you! You may think you were sacked unfairly and this may be the case, but one of the rules of the interview game is that you don't run down ex-bosses (or teachers, or examining boards) to an

interviewer. Think through why you were sacked. Was it through some behaviour that you have now changed, eg unpunctuality? Was it because you lacked skills that you have now gained or are willing to learn?

A 'I had just left school when I took that job and my parents were getting divorced. I had so much to cope with that I became rather unreliable at work and they didn't keep me on after my three months' probation period. But things have settled down now and I'm back to my old self. You can see from my school references that I'm usually a very reliable person.'

Why?
You have told the interviewer:

➡➡ that you accept responsibility for the difficulties, rather than blaming other people
➡➡ you were working under exceptionally difficult circumstances
➡➡ you are now working well and can prove it

Q 'Why did you fail your maths exam?'

What is the interviewer trying to find out?
Simply, your reason for not passing the exam. The interviewer will not know whether it was because you dislike maths, had a poor teacher, had an off day during the exam, are not good at maths or for another reason.

A 'I was very disappointed not to pass my maths exam because it's a subject I'm quite good at. However, I can only blame myself – I made a poor choice of what to revise and this left me with a few questions I felt less than confident about.'

Why?
Again, don't lie – if you're not good at maths or don't like it, don't pretend otherwise. However, there is no need to

actually point out your dislike or inability. Simply tell the interviewer that you had failed to revise enough, or whatever the reason might be.

In this answer the interviewer is told that:

➡➡ you like maths and normally do well at this subject,
➡➡ you accept responsibility for your own mistakes
➡➡ you can learn from your mistakes.

Of course, if you failed because a teacher was ill for a considerable time or part of the coursework was not covered you should say so. If this is the case and you are applying to university, ask your headteacher to mention this in your reference letter. Do this also if maths (or whatever subject you are considering) is relevant to the job you are applying for.

Q 'I can't see anything in your form for last year. What were you doing then?'

What is the interviewer trying to find out?
Simply, why there is a gap in your application form.

A 'Well, after I'd finished my GCSEs I tried to find a job as a secretary. I didn't have much luck. I couldn't get accepted for Youth Training locally because so few companies are offering places and although I applied for over 20 jobs I was unsuccessful. Most of them wanted experience, which of course I don't have, so it's a bit of a Catch 22 situation. I've got a typewriter at home so I did practise my skills and can type 50 words per minute now. Also, I did some typing for a charity my aunt is involved in. I've realised now, though, that I need more qualifications and that's why I'm applying for this course.'

Why?
You haven't emphasised the fact that you were out of work, although this is, of course, implied. You have, however, shown that:

- ➥ you tried hard to get a job or a place on a scheme
- ➥ you were motivated enough to practise and improve your typing skills
- ➥ you were willing to use those skills for the charity (good experience that you can talk about)
- ➥ you have considered your future and are acting responsibly by applying for further training

Exercise

On a sheet of paper, write a list of the questions you don't want to be asked and how you would answer them. Keep the sheet in your interview file.

I asked this candidate why I should give her the job. She was silent for a while and then proceeded to tell me all the things she had failed at during

her secretarial course. She
would have done much better
to tell me all the things she
did well, or at least keep quiet
about the failures!

,

*Quote from a manager interviewing an applicant for
a secretarial vacancy*

Your question time

Well, that's it, question time over.

Just a minute though, there's always those last few
minutes when the interviewer says 'Are there any
questions you'd like to ask?' And what happens? Your
mind goes a complete blank. Don't worry, you can
prepare for your own questions just as you can prepare
for theirs.

And do prepare a sensible, well-thought-out question
or two. A lecturer at an HE college tells me that she often
gets asked 'Is there much writing/reading on this course?'
Well, naturally there is on any higher education course!
Another irritating question is 'How many hours a week
will I have to work at home?' This shows a lack of
commitment to the course right from the start.

DO NOT ask whether the buses will get you to the
college on time. And I promise you, I'm not joking. A lot
of interviewees seem more interested in this than in the
course. You are an adult – find out about the buses
yourself.

If it's a job you're being interviewed for, it's bad form
to ask about pay, car loans, holidays, and so forth at the
interview. You can ask these questions when they phone
to offer you the job – you'll be bargaining from a position
of strength then. You can read more about this in
Chapter 12.

But here are some typical end of interview questions that won't be frowned on or make you look mercenary.

1. When can I expect to hear if I've got the job/place?
2. Who would supervise me?
3. What training will I be offered?
4. How will my success be measured?
5. What career/research opportunities might arise in the future?
6. Can you tell me more about this aspect of the course/job?
7. What percentage of time is spent on . . .?
8. Are there any new developments likely in the organisation of the company?

A couple of extra questions you might like to consider if you feel confident about handling them are:

- 'What qualities do you want from the person you see in this job?'

This gives you an opportunity to check if you've given the right information about yourself. If the interviewer mentions qualities you've already told them you've got, you can smile and say (modestly!) something like 'That doesn't seem too difficult.' If, on the other hand, they mention qualities you haven't yet discussed, you have a last opportunity to sell yourself.

- 'What problems do you think this area of work might involve?'

Only ask this if you can reasonably anticipate what the answer might be. That way, you can make suggestions and you'll impress the interviewer no end. If you're taken by surprise, you may need to make a more non-committal answer, such as 'That's interesting', and hope they don't press you to elaborate.

If you are applying for jobs and can afford to be choosy about which one you accept, you may want to ask more probing questions than this. For example, if you want to know what makes your prospective boss tick, you can ask about his or her leisure interests. If your boss hasn't any, does this mean he/she is a workaholic who will expect you to work all hours? Will you mind if so?

If you think that you'll forget your questions, write them down. Then you can refer to them as necessary. This looks efficient, not forgetful.

Should the interviewer have covered every question you had thought of, it's perfectly acceptable to simply say 'Well, I had a number of questions when I arrived, but you've covered all of them, I don't think there's anything else. Thank you.'

BUT, there's one last question you should always ask and that is whether you are likely to be given the place/job. This feels awkward for most people and you shouldn't ask outright, but if you word it as 'Am I the sort of person you are looking for?' the interviewer may give you a yes or no. Or, if you're lucky, depending on how you look at it, they may say something along the lines of 'Well, we were looking for someone with more experience of . . .'. This gives you an opportunity to sell yourself further by over-coming any shortcomings in your apparent suitability.

Exercise

Make a list of questions you can ask at the interview. Remember to consider what you have learnt about the company or college from your research. The interviewer will be impressed if it is clear that you have bothered to do your homework.

Chapter Checklist

❏ **Do you feel confident that you can explain away those awkward facts about yourself (if they apply)?**
  ➡ lack of skills
  ➡ lack of experience
  ➡ lack of qualifications
  ➡ lack of interests
  ➡ poor work history
  ➡ gaps in your CV
  ➡ your habit of giving up on things
  ➡ why you failed some courses

❏ **Have you worked out how to present your answers in the best possible light?**

❏ **Have you made a list of questions to ask at the end of the interview?**
  ➡ you can ask for further details of course/supervisors/career openings
  ➡ you can ask about pensions
  ➡ you can ask about line management
  ➡ avoid asking about holidays or salary until offered the job
  ➡ you can ask when you will hear the result of your interview

❏ **Remember to take a smartly written list of questions with you into the interview – a scruffy piece of paper won't do.**

❏ **Don't be afraid to say so if the interviewer has already answered all your questions, but let him or her know that you had some prepared.**

4 Emotional Preparation

You should read this chapter:

- ➡ well in advance of your interview. Many of the methods of overcoming nerves require practice to be effective

By the end of this chapter you should know:

- ➡ why a certain amount of nervousness can be helpful in an interview
- ➡ a range of methods to help you to feel calm during the interview
- ➡ how these methods work

If you feel nervous facing an interview, you're not alone. It is not at all unusual to feel sick, have butterflies in your stomach, blush, stutter, have your mind go blank or to experience any other of a dozen physical reactions to a stressful situation.

 We always allow for students' nervousness – in fact we assume that they are nervous.

Quote from a college interviewer

In fact, a bit of extra adrenalin is just what you need. After all, an interview is an artificial situation, with unspoken but well-recognised rules played by both sides. A reasonable amount of adrenalin gives you that sharp edge to perform a bit better than usual – ask any actor. But too much fear (and too much adrenalin) has the opposite effect. It stops you thinking clearly, and this is a time when you want your mind to be particularly clear, when you don't want to feel as if you might gag. So you need to work on eliminating or at least lessening those unwanted feelings. The good news is that just as you can prepare for any other aspect of an interview, you can prepare yourself to keep calm.

Here are a few techniques. They all have three things in common:

- ➥ they distract you momentarily from the stressful feelings
- ➥ they allow you to slow down your breathing; most people breathe more shallowly and faster when they are nervous, and
- ➥ they give you back a feeling of control

Select the one which you think might work best for you and practise until the calming reaction becomes automatic. Practise is the key. It is no good leaving it until the interview itself to use one of these techniques. Although it may well help, if you rehearse the method thoroughly in advance it will have a far greater impact.

To do this, select a safe place and time and begin to think about a stressful situation (the interview?) or watch a horror film, or seek out a spider, or whatever turns you off. Then use one of the techniques to calm yourself. Try to really capture the feeling of being in control of yourself and the situation. Strengthen your breathing, sit in a more upright way, feel strong, feel personally powerful feel good about yourself. If you do this enough times, the calming reaction becomes automatic and you can 'switch into' calm mode whenever you need to.

If you're a bit sceptical about this, remember that you weren't born being nervous of interviews. You learn to react in certain ways as your experiences of situations work on your personality. In the same way you can unlearn these nuisance feelings, leaving you feeling in control. It works, try it!

Often people are so nervous that they don't hear my questions properly. This means that they waffle on, missing the point entirely.

Quote from a manager with extensive interviewing experience

Anchoring

This is a great technique, very simple and effective. With one hand, hold your other wrist. As you do so, say to yourself 'calm, calm', and become aware of your breathing. Slow your breathing down. Feel in control.

Do try this one, it has several advantages:

- barring amputation, you will always have your wrist with you
- the action is unobtrusive
- you can hold your wrist comfortably whether sitting down, standing up, or holding documents

Be careful, of course, that you don't grip your wrist so tightly that your fingers fall off from lack of blood! As with the other examples here, over time you can learn to associate this technique with feeling calm. In a stressful situation taking hold of your wrist will trigger feeling calm.

By the way, you don't have to say 'calm', it can be anything that works for you. Some of the suggestions in the section below might be effective for you.

Self-talk

If you are feeling panicky, it's likely that all sorts of negative feelings are going through your mind.

'Help, I'm going to be sick!'

'I'll make a right mess of this.'

'What if I can't answer the questions?'

'Why did this big zit have to come up today of all days?'

'Why am I here?'

All perfectly natural. The thing to remember is that you can take control of these feelings. After all, if you're not in control of your mind, who is?

So, start adjusting your self-talk. Stop the negative thoughts and replace them with positive ones.

'I can handle this.'

'Interviews are a good opportunity for me to find out about the college/job.'

'They don't want me to fail, and I won't.'

'I feel good today. I'm in control.'

'I'm an okay person.'

As you think these positive thoughts, adjust your body language. Negative thoughts tend to mean that we slump. Lift your head, square your shoulders and take a few deep breaths. It's okay, it'll be all right, you can do it.

In fact, you could get the interviewer on your side by owning up to your nervousness. If you feel really nervous and think that you look like a quivering wreck, own up. Simply say, briefly 'I always feel nervous during interviews.'

INNER SELF-TALK

Negative self-talk

poor self-image

'loser' body language, and
lack of confidence in interview

weak performance at interview

Positive self-talk

strong self-image

'winner' body language, and
confidence in interview

good performance at interview

Grounding

Grounding is a bit like anchoring. The idea is to distract your thoughts away from the stressful situation towards a calm feeling. With this technique, you deliberately become conscious of your body weight through the seat of the chair or through your feet. Try it now as you read this page. You don't usually think about it, do you, but it's easy once you focus your attention.

Once you've become conscious of your body weight (no, not how fat you are!), think to yourself 'calm, calm', slow down your breathing and take control again.

Visualising

This is a great one if you're good at fantasies. In your mind's eye conjure up a soothing picture. It might be a lovely scene from your holiday, a flower, a waterfall, whatever. With this image firmly in your mind, if only for a split second, slow down your breathing and think to yourself 'calm, calm'. Take control, feel on top of the situation.

When you practise using this technique, concentrate on the soothing quality of your chosen image to help you feel calm.

Imaging

This is one you've probably learnt from your grannie. Imagine the interviewer in his or her underwear. It's a wonderful leveller, and they won't seem nearly so imposing without the smart business suit.

My grannie used to remind me as well 'Just remember, they all go to the toilet the same as us' – another great leveller.

Try it now!

So, what have you got to lose but your fear? Try it out, you'll feel foolish the first few times, but if you practise when you're alone, no one will know.

Chapter Checklist

Do you feel confident that you:

- ❏ can anticipate at what stage you are likely to feel nervous?

- ❏ will recognise the warning signs when they appear?

- ❏ understand how calming methods work?

- ❏ have tried the various methods to establish which one works for you?

- ❏ have practised your chosen method until you automatically respond by:
  - ➻ slowing your breathing?
  - ➻ breathing more deeply?
  - ➻ feeling in control?

Pat's Story

'I was asked to act as guinea pig for some middle-ranking civil servants on a selection-interviewing course. I had been in my post about two months and they asked me to act as if I were being interviewed for the job for the first time. I went into the room feeling fairly relaxed, after all, I already had the job. I came out a wreck. The interviewers didn't ask me any settling-in questions and immediately asked me very technical questions about aspects of my work that I knew I'd never have to deal with in a month of Sundays. They were just showing off in front of each other, and being really arrogant. I know that I didn't put myself across very well. The feedback was that they'd have given me the job but on minimum salary – no extra increments.

'The second interview was several hours later. What a difference. The whole thing was much more relaxed and informal. They made sure I felt settled and asked me sensible and relevant questions. I left the room feeling good about myself, knowing I'd let them know what I could do. I got feedback that not only would they have employed me, but they'd have given me several extra increments too. There was no way I could have increased my knowledge of my job in that time – it was simply their attitudes that made the difference.'

5 **Practical Preparation**

You should read this chapter:

●+ as soon as you are offered an interview

By the end of this chapter you should know:

●+ what to consider when planning your journey to the interview
●+ what you should take to the interview
●+ how to dress appropriately
●+ issues to consider when taking a parent to the interview

So far we've looked at mental and emotional preparation for the interview. Let's look now at more practical matters. You have been invited to attend an interview. What do you need to consider?

The place

Do you know where the college or organisation is? How will you get there? If you need to use public transport, what bus/train do you catch? What is the timetable? How long does it take? If you are driving, can you use their car park? Phone first, if you're not sure.

Remember to allow yourself plenty of travel time. The last thing you want is to spend the journey anxiously looking at your watch and feeling panicky. And a definite minus point in most interviewers' books is to arrive late. After all, if you do that at an interview, what would you be like once you got the job?

This is also true of college interviews. True, many tutors are surprised if people turn up for lectures at all, never mind late, but on the interview day they're likely to be working flat out trying to stay on schedule.

What to take

You may have been asked to take some things with you, for example proof of qualifications or references.

There will probably be some other things you would like to take. For job interviews these might include:

- ➤ a copy of your application form, CV, Record of Achievement, certificates, portfolio
- ➤ a list of questions to ask at the end of the interview
- ➤ details about the organisation – so that you can re-read them if you're kept waiting
- ➤ anything which would be likely to boost your chances of success. Though if you must take your lucky teddy bear, please keep it hidden!

For a college interview, you should definitely take:

- ➤ Record of Achievement, GNVQ portfolio (if you have been taking GNVQs), certificates
- ➤ samples of any appropriate work
- ➤ details about the course and college

For either type of interview you should also prepare everyday things:

- ➤ handkerchief or clean tissues. Scrunched-up pink loo paper is less than impressive!
- ➤ specs if you need them
- ➤ money (including some change for the phone, in case you get held up and need to let them know you'll be late)
- ➤ timetable or parking instructions
- ➤ an umbrella if there's the least chance of rain. It's hard to make a good impression with water dripping down your neck.
- ➤ a comb
- ➤ the name and telephone number of the interviewer in case of delays

Women might like to add to this list:

- spare pairs of tights/stockings
- sanitary protection

Stress, journeys and Sod's law being what they are, you might well need one or the other . . .

A word of warning. Find something suitable, APPROPRIATE, to carry these things in. If you don't have, and can't borrow, a briefcase or similar, an envelope file looks smart.

Believe it or not, I have seen people turn up for interviews with what appears to be their week's shopping in Tesco's bags. If you absolutely, positively have to carry something (such as the umbrella) that you don't want to take into the interview, leave it with the receptionist.

Overnight stays

Many interviews, especially for college places, will involve you travelling to another part of the country. What does this involve? Well, imagine yourself in a strange town, one hour before the interview, discovering that the only shoes you've got to wear with your smart outfit are your trainers . . . Doesn't bear thinking about, does it?

So planning is all. Make a list of EVERYTHING you're likely to need a couple of days before you set out. This gives you time to buy or borrow any missing items. Here are some suggestions:

- outfit
- underwear
- toothbrush
- hairdryer
- tissues
- directions
- letter of invitation
- towel
- shoes
- toothpaste
- shampoo
- comb
- money
- documents
- pyjamas
- map

- ➼ book
- ➼ alarm clock
- ➼ prepared list of questions and answers
- ➼ pen
- ➼ medicines
- ➼ perfume/aftershave
- ➼ razor

This sort of careful preparation leaves your mind free to concentrate on important matters.

Looking the part

Okay, so here you are, well organised. You know where you're going, how to get there and what you need to take. Now you have to decide what to wear.

This is a subject that can arouse strong emotions. People say that it's not what you look like but what you do that is important. Absolutely true. BUT while one part of our mind knows that, the rest of our mind works differently. Many experts on interviewer-training say that the interviewer unconsciously decides within the first 90 seconds whether or not they like a candidate. Then they spend the rest of the interview justifying their decision.

 I interviewed one woman who turned up in a pink fluffy trouser suit. She'd only have needed ears to look like a toy bunny!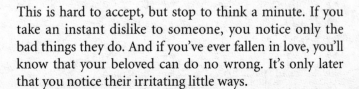

Quote from an interviewer

This is hard to accept, but stop to think a minute. If you take an instant dislike to someone, you notice only the bad things they do. And if you've ever fallen in love, you'll know that your beloved can do no wrong. It's only later that you notice their irritating little ways.

Also, keep in mind that many interviewers are not trained, and that many of them are walking bags of prejudice. Unfortunately, there is nothing you can do about this from outside the organisation, but once you've got a place on the course, or got the job you want, you can work to change things from inside.

 We're looking at the whole person and dress presents part of the overall pattern. If they dress untidily, it may mean they think untidily.

Quote from a college interviewer

'But,' you may be thinking 'I don't have many clothes and no money to buy more.' Do the best you can with what you've got. Look through your possible outfits, keeping in mind 'What does the sort of person who already does the job/attend the course I'm looking for wear?' This doesn't matter quite so much for students, although there are few lecturers who relish the thought of teaching someone who's dirty and smelly.

Looking right is very important, however, if you're applying for a job, and the comments below relate more to job interviews.

For example, if you're going for a job as a garage mechanic and you're lucky enough to have a £500 suit complete with flash silk tie and portable phone, you might look a bit over the top. No interviewer wants to feel inferior beside the candidate!

So, dress smartly and neatly. This is no time for extremes of fashion, unless you're going for a job where it's appropriate, such as in a trendy fashion shop. You need to look sensible, reliable and, above all, employable.

Appearance matters

Okay, now you've looked at your wardrobe and selected the best you can. Whatever you choose, inspect it carefully. Are any repairs needed? Is it clean? It's no good noticing as you dress for the big occasion that there's a gravy stain down the front. Get the outfit ready well in advance and remember:

- look clean and tidy
- have shoes polished and repaired, even if they're old
- have clean hair
- smell okay – no body odour or bad breath
- don't overdo the perfume or aftershave
- look appropriate for the season – I once interviewed someone who was wearing a very thick tartan suit on a very hot summer day. For this and other reasons she didn't get the job.

Gender differences

The general impression you are trying to give with your clothing is of someone who is capable and efficient. Of course, all of this is easier for the guys. A suit or smart trousers and jacket or jumper will carry them through most types of interview.

The choice is much harder for a woman though. The same guidelines still apply. But women also need to consider:

- **trousers** I know it's not fair or right, but some employers are still prejudiced against them. Get the job and then tackle the sexism.
- **make-up** It's fine to wear it, but if you usually wear heavy make-up, consider if it's what women who are already doing the job would wear.
- **shoes** Try to work out what the interview might cover. If, for example, you are planning to wear very high heels and the interview will include a walk round a building site, will you manage?

Hobbling does nothing for your dignity.

- **jewellery** Again, avoid extremes and anything jingly that might distract the interviewer from listening to what you have to say.
- **comfort** If you've bought something new, wear it before the interview for an hour or so. Is it comfortable? Does the skirt ride up when you sit down? Remember, if you feel uncomfortable, you're likely to do less well in the interview.
- **cardigans** Try to avoid the dreaded cardigan, unless it's very smart. A jacket gives a much more polished impression.
- **too many bags** If you're taking a briefcase, try not to take a handbag as well. You may get in a muddle when you have to put all these things down and pick them up. You'll have enough other things to think about.

Mum's the word – or is she?

Whilst it's rare for young people to take their parents along to a job interview, they do sometimes take them to a college interview, especially at higher education colleges, and also to Youth Training interviews. There's nothing right or wrong about this, but you may want to give it some thought.

About 50 per cent of them bring their parents along to the interview. I've seen some of my colleagues forget who's applying for the course and interview parents instead.

Quote from a regional college lecturer about interviewing prospective students

Yes, it's sad but true that interviewers are human and get it wrong occasionally, like forgetting to speak to you when there's a parent there. So, when considering whether to take along a parent keep in mind:

- ➔ Will you cringe when your friends see their old-fashioned clothes?
- ➔ Are they domineering types who won't let you get a word in edgeways?
- ➔ Do they think they know more than the lecturer about the subject?

On a more serious note, if you do take a parent along, discuss with them beforehand what their role is to be. It is awkward for interviewers who are faced with you plus parent(s) to have to ask or guess who is actually going into the interview room. Furthermore, if a parent is going into the interview room with you, decide whether they are going to sit silently unless asked to comment or whether they can feel free to join in.

Chapter Checklist

Do you feel confident about:

❏ **how you will get to the interview?**
  ➠ parking
  ➠ timetables
  ➠ time for emergencies
  ➠ overnight stays

❏ **what to take into the interview room?**
  ➠ bag
  ➠ briefcase
  ➠ folder

❏ **what to take for an overnight stay, if this is necessary?**

❏ **what to take it in?**

❏ **what to wear?**
  ➠ smart and appropriate are key words

❏ **that your outfit is clean and tidy?**
  ➠ do running repairs, polish shoes

❏ **that your accessories are not distracting?**
  ➠ nothing jangly, or too eye-catching

❏ **that you haven't overdone the perfume or aftershave?**

❏ **whether or not to take a parent?**

❏ **the role the parent or parents will play in the interview?**

6 Presenting your GNVQ portfolio and Record of Achievement

You should read this chapter:

➼ as soon as you are offered an interview

By the end of this chapter you should know:

➼ how to present your GNVQ portfolio and/or National Record of Achievement
➼ how to select relevant material to show at interview
➼ how to use your projects to demonstrate that you are the right person for the job or college place for which you are applying

If you have been invited to attend an interview, you will already have told the interviewer something about your qualifications, skills and personality on your application form or CV. You should, of course, be ready to answer questions about what you have written there. Chapter two will help you with this if you are still unsure of how to shape your answers.

But that's not all. There is other evidence you can present at the actual interview which, used well, should impress the interviewer no end. In this chapter we'll look at two major sources of evidence of your brilliance. The first, your National Record of Achievement, is something that most school leavers now have. The second, a portfolio of GNVQ work, applies only if you have taken this qualification.

Preparation

Put yourself in your interviewer's shoes. Which would impress you most: a scruffy, muddled portfolio or one that is tidy, ordered and pleasing to the eye? No contest. So set aside a few hours sometime in the week before your interview to check through your Record of Achievement or GNVQ portfolio. Follow these tips to save panic on the day of the interview.

- Make sure everything is organised, tidy and appealing to look at.
- Make sure nothing vital is missing. If you haven't looked at your Record of Achievement or GNVQ portfolio for a while, it's easy to forget that you took something out for some reason.
- Make sure your Record of Achievement or GNVQ portfolio is in a sensible order and you know where everything is in it. Bear in mind that the interviewer may express an interest in something you hadn't planned to discuss – so you need to know what's where.
- If you have a Record of Achievement *and* GNVQ portfolio some things, such as an action plan, may be included in both. Don't worry about this, but make sure that both are up to date.
- Mark the items you want to show with sticky 'post-it' notes so you can find them quickly. Alternatively, you might want to collect these items at the front, so you won't have to hunt for them at all.

The next points depend on whether it is your Record of Achievement or a GNVQ portfolio that you are a showing.

Using your National Record of Achievement

Your Record of Achievement will consist of a folder containing most if not all of these standard sheets:

- ◆▸ **Personal details** – including address and education/training history
- ◆▸ **Personal statement** – your chance to bring to attention your strong points
- ◆▸ **Employment history** – details of jobs you have had
- ◆▸ **Qualifications and credits** – your vocational and academic qualifications, or credits towards them
- ◆▸ **Achievements and experiences** – activities outside school, such as social or community work, a first aid certificate, sporting awards, etc
- ◆▸ **Individual action plan** – helping you to plan the next stage of your development

In addition, if you are still at school you will have a sheet for **School achievements** – including positions of responsibility (eg prefect, captain of school team) – and **Attendance rate**.

If you have evidence to support some of your claims, in the form of exam certificates, references, letters and signed statements, put them in the folder too.

Looking through your folder will help prepare you to explain where you are now and your goals for the future. The document will also tell your interviewer quite a lot about your personality and your life to date. Before you go to the interview, do the same sort of brainstorming exercise as on page 16 to think about what your achievements demonstrate. For instance:

- ◆▸ Visiting and talking to old folk one afternoon a week shows you are caring and good at getting on with different kinds of people.
- ◆▸ Playing in the county tennis team meant you had to give up your Sunday morning lie-in for the summer, but you made every coaching session, so you are reliable. It also shows you have determination – the selection process was tough.

➡ Taking the evening class for the life-saver's award shows you have self-motivation. (You had no need to do it, but you decided you wanted to.)

➡ Organising the scout trip to Wales shows your leadership ability and your ability to cope in a crisis. (The van broke down half way up the M4. You had to call a mechanic, find a Youth Hostel for the group to stay in that night, and negotiate for an extra day's tuition from your climbing instructor.)

➡ Editing the newsletter for your local sports club shows your ability to write and your organisational skills. (You had to chase all the other contributors for their articles.)

So don't be afraid to blow your own trumpet, even about small things – it may be that the company you apply to is short of a person qualified to give first aid (or whatever your extra skill is), and that could swing the decision in your favour.

Presenting a GNVQ portfolio

If you have been taking a GNVQ, you will have gathered lots of evidence about the work you have done during your course. Depending on your subject, your portfolio may include:

➡ sketches and drawings, photos

➡ written reports

➡ graphs and charts

➡ video recordings of presentations you made

➡ a diary describing projects you carried out on work experience

➡ a log book recording your thoughts about what you have learnt

➡ notes for a talk you gave to younger pupils

➡ results from a survey of local employers

In fact, there will be such a lot of material in your GNVQ portfolio that you must be selective, and take only a small portion of it to your interview. It will be no good if you overwhelm the interviewer, or if you are so busy sorting through piles of paper that you can't concentrate on the questions you are being asked!

Be selective

So how do you choose which bits of your portfolio to take with you to the interview? Obviously you want to choose what you consider to be your best pieces of work. But you must also ask yourself what the interviewer is most likely to be interested in. Suppose last year you completed a Foundation level GNVQ in Health and Social Care. Now you are applying for a job as a care assistant in an old people's home. There is likely to be some work you did in unit 2 (Understanding personal development and relationships) and in unit 3 (Investigating working in health and social care) that will be relevant.

Alternatively, you may be applying for a degree course in Marketing to follow on from your Advanced GNVQ in Business. Take with you your work on preparing a marketing plan from unit 8 (Business planning), and some projects from unit 3 (Marketing).

Or suppose the job you are applying for is a junior designer position in a company that produces corporate brochures. In that case you are likely to have a wide choice of work to show from your Advanced GNVQ in Art and Design. You might take one project from the unit on 2-D visual design, one showing how you investigated working to design briefs, and one about business practice.

Try to find just three or four projects that will cover what you want to say. You will rarely have the opportunity to talk for longer than that will allow. But with that many projects you are still likely to have something relevant with you if the interviewer asks a 'Have you ever done anything about . . . ?' question.

> Students should select and present at interview a small sample of evidence from their portfolio to illustrate key aspects relevant to their applications. Students must also be prepared to discuss any evidence they take to the interview. Lack of understanding of the materials presented cast doubt on the authenticity of the evidence.

Lessons from the first phase of Advanced GNVQ applicants to higher education, GATE project, October 1994

Think through what you will say about your material

As we've seen in earlier chapters, you can really prepare yourself well for an interview by anticipating questions. So try to think of everything the interviewer could ask about your projects. Some typical questions might be:

1. Why did you choose to focus on . . . ?
2. How did you find out about . . . ?
3. How did you organise so many people to . . . ?
4. Did the results of your survey surprise you?
5. If you had to do the project again now, what would you do differently?
6. What did you learn from keeping a log book?
7. Did you all work well together as a team?
8. What was your contribution to the project?

That last question is important, by the way. If one of the projects you are going to talk about was carried out in a group with other people, make sure you can describe the bit of the work that was done by you! If you are claiming to have done this work and you can't talk about it when questioned, any interviewer is going to be suspicious.

> Often people tell me what their team achieved, but when asked what THEY did, they don't seem able to answer, even when pressed.

A manager

By the way, bear in mind that GNVQ is a new qualification and your interviewer may not know much about it – you may find yourself having to explain how it works. For some ideas of how to do this, see page 48.

Chapter Checklist

❏ Is your portfolio/Record of Achievement neat and tidy, and up to date? Do you know where everything is in it?

❏ Have you thought about how you will use your portfolio/Record of Achievement to sell yourself?

❏ Have you picked out the parts of your portfolio/Record of Achievement that will most interest your interviewer?

❏ Have you thought through what you will say about the material you have chosen?

❏ Have you thought about questions the interviewer might ask about your portfolio/Record of Achievement?

2

The Successful Interview

7 Types of Interview

You should read this chapter:

➻ preferably no later than one week before the interview

By the end of this chapter you should know:

➻ the different types of interview you may face
➻ why interviewers use different types of interview

Into the torture chamber

Well, I hope by now you're convinced that an interview need not be a sophisticated form of torture, after all. An interview is a two-way process – an opportunity for the interviewer to find out about you and for you to find out more about the college or job you are applying for. Approaching an interview from this perspective gives a much more balanced view and gives you back a sense of control. Having said that, you need to be aware that there are interviews and interviews. If you haven't been told what type of interview you will be facing when you arrive, don't hesitate to phone first to ask. It's okay to do so, and you owe it to yourself to be as well informed as possible.

One-to-one interviews

As the name suggests, a one-to-one interview is when you face just one interviewer working alone. This is often the case when you apply for a relatively low-level job, and for some college courses.

This is probably the least stressful type of interview (from your point of view), as you only have to relate to one person. The disadvantage is that there is only one person's view of you, and if that's unfavourable, there is no one else to challenge it.

Occasionally, you may be faced with a series of one-to-one interviews. Colleges or organisations may do this when, for example, you would be working or studying in several different departments, or when different people are needed to explain different aspects of the job or course.

One-to-two or -three interviews

This is a very common format, both for job and college interviews. It is slightly more difficult for you to relate to more than one person, but two or three is not too bad.

Probably your most difficult task is deciding who to look at. There's a simple rule. Look mostly at the person who asked you the question, but shift your gaze from time to time to take in the other people. You probably do this without thinking when talking to friends, but self-consciousness in an interview often robs us of our natural body language. Next time you're with two or three friends, practise until you can comfortably handle appropriate eye contact.

The advantage of this type of interview is that there are several opinions of you which will give a more measured view.

Panel interviews

It is unlikely that you will be facing a panel interview at this stage in your career, but it is worth being aware of them just in case.

In a panel interview you will be facing a whole heap of people. Interviewers may use this style when they want to share the decision for some reason. Alternatively, they may wish to appoint someone who will work with all of them, and therefore they will want to have a say in the final choice made. This is a common interview style for teachers who can face as many as 14 interviewers (so feel sorry for them after all!).

If you are faced with more than three people, it can be difficult to keep them all in view at the same time. This is especially true as the more of them there are, the further away you are likely to be seated, because they all need to be able to see you too. As before, the trick is to give most attention to the person asking the question. However, you must look at the other interviewers. If there are too many people to look at individually, you can look at them in groups of three or four. Try it at a party sometime, it does work.

Group interviews

These can take any one of a number of forms. Group interviews are sometimes used in addition to a one-to-one or one-to-two interview. In this scenario, the group are not candidates (although they may be together), but a group already existing at the college or workplace. The purpose of this type of interview is to give this team of people an opportunity to meet the candidate they will work with and to pass on their thoughts. Alternatively, it is for observers to check out your group behaviour, or what you say. Here are some variations on this theme:

1 Meet the team members

In this type of group interview candidates are placed in different rooms, alone, and existing members of staff will wander from room to room chatting to each of the candidates. This can appear to be a fairly relaxed and informal procedure. Don't be fooled – unless you are told otherwise, assume that it's part of the formal process – it usually is.

2 Questions in a row

This type of interview is again often used in conjunction with a one-to-one or one-to-two interview. In this scenario the candidates are put together in a room, and are each asked the same questions, which they have to answer in front of each other. Yetch! The problem is, if you go first and then someone else comes up with a better answer, you'll kick yourself for not thinking of it. If you go last, there's sometimes nothing left to say. There's no way round it, you just have to do your best. After all, with the thorough preparation you have done, you'll be okay. Comfort yourself with the thought that the other candidates have the same problem.

3 Group task

Occasionally, you may be asked to work with other candidates to solve a problem. This is not unusual in interviews for officership in the armed forces. The task is likely to be something that should show the observers:

- ➨ how you behave as a team member
- ➨ how innovative you are
- ➨ whether you display leadership qualities
- ➨ how you think on your feet

If you know that you are going for this type of interview, it is unlikely that you will be told in advance what the task is and this makes preparation difficult. However, you might consider looking at a book on leadership skills or trying to talk to other people who do similar work to see what pointers you can get.

Some of the candidates seemed completely thrown at having to join in a group discussion. They slumped in their chairs and this gave a very poor impression.

Quote from a manager interviewing candidates for a senior post

4 Group discussion

This method can be used both in job and college interviews. All the candidates are seated together, usually round a table, and are given a topic or case-study to discuss.

The purpose of the discussion is for the observers to learn more about you. It is worth keeping in mind that negative qualities displayed by people in groups are:

- aggression
- domination
- stubbornness
- criticism
- prejudice

- rudeness
- silence
- interrupting
- poor listening
- ignoring others

Positive qualities and behaviours include:

- summarising
- consideration for others
- keeping to the topic
- flexibility
- good body language

- sharing ideas
- contributing regularly to the discussion
- humour (but not too much)
- encouraging others
- listening

For example, if you are applying for a job that involves negotiating or attending a lot of meetings, you may well be given a topic to discuss which should demonstrate your skills in these areas.

Discussion topics will obviously vary according to the organisation and the job or college place you are applying for, but here are some typical examples.

- Discuss where this organisation (or service) will be in five years' time.
- Discuss the role this organisation can play in the future of...
- What do you think the main problems facing... are today?
- How could... be improved?

If, however, you are applying for a place on, say, a social work course, it is more likely that the observers will be checking out your attitudes. You may, for example, be asked to discuss:

- ➥ the priorities which should be given to distributing a limited budget to various needy groups (some at least will be controversial)
- ➥ the best way to help a particular client group

There are endless variations on the group interview, these are just some suggestions so that you get a feel for what to expect. Don't forget though, that you can ask for at least a rough idea of what is likely to be involved in the whole interview process before the big day.

Internal interviews

These may happen if you are:

- ➥ going for another job where you already work
- ➥ trying to change course part of the way through your time at college/university
- ➥ applying to take a higher qualification at your existing college

One problem with internal interviews is that you can fail to take them seriously. This may be because you know the set-up inside out, share your coffee breaks with the interviewer, feel embarrassed because they know you (warts and all) or simply feel over-confident. DON'T. Treat this interview as seriously as any other. Don't slouch, make in-jokes, moan about difficult people you both know. Remember, if there is competition for the job or place, the other candidates will be trying hard to put on a polished performance – can you afford to do less? I don't think so!

The second problem is that people know you too well, and have preconceived ideas about you. It may be that you will have to work hard to overcome some prejudices on their part. Again, treat the interview as seriously as any other, considering all the points you need to raise to sell yourself effectively.

Informal interviews

You may just be asked to attend a lunch or go to a pub with the existing work team or students, so that they can meet you. This may be a truly informal meeting with no feedback to the formal interviewers or it may actually be part of the formal process in disguise. Either way, just be yourself, use your preparation and DON'T DRINK ALCOHOL no matter how tempted you may be.

Agency interviews

Employment agencies have vacancies for all types of jobs, although many specialise in one particular area – for example, in secretarial or catering staff. If you have sent your CV to an agency, they may either call you in for a general interview straightaway, or they may wait and call you for an interview for a particular post when they think you have the skills and/or qualifications one of their client companies needs.

If it is a particular post you are being considered for, you will often have the first interview with the agency rather than the actual employer. (The agencies save the employers time and effort by selecting only a few very suitable people to be sent to the employer for interview.) You should prepare for this interview in the same way as you would for any other. Find out beforehand from the agency as much as you can about the job and about the employer.

If, on the other hand, you are called for a general interview, this is a different affair. You should tell the agency about ALL the skills you have. After all, you never know what job they might have coming up next week and your experience three years ago at the riding stable might just come in handy. Be prepared, too, to be tested quite thoroughly on your skills if you are offering to do temping work in secretarial duties. There may be many many people with similar skills to you, so competition could be fierce.

Agencies interviews are usually less formal than other interviews. But don't be too relaxed! You want to come across as professional enough for the agency to be happy about recommending you to any of their clients. By the way, most agency interviews are one to one.

Finally, a warning. It has been known for an agency interview for a specific job to change in the course of the half hour into a general interview (or even an interview for a *different* job!). This might happen if they discover you have some extra skills they didn't know about which make you better suited for another post. Or alternatively they may just want to get to know you better, so they can consider you for anything else that comes up if you don't make this job. Be prepared!

Advertised interviews

Sometimes you will see companies advertising that they will be interviewing people for jobs at a certain place on a particular day. These often seem to be sales jobs and the interviews are frequently held in hotels. You may not be expected to ring for an interview but check the wording of the advertisement. You simply turn up on the day and wait to be seen.

All companies run these differently. Some will do a formal interview on that day, whilst others will simply tell you about the job, and give you a form to take the application further if you are interested.

Hidden interviews

Some employers are really sneaky. They'll send you off on a tour of the office, factory or whatever with an underling. You chat away innocently, saying how terrified you are at interviews, how you really haven't got half the skills they're after, or, worse still, you treat the underling with less than the respect they deserve. And what happens? Prior to your formal interview they feed all this back to the interviewer.

So, if you're asked to take part in anything of this nature, be friendly, polite and interested. Do not disclose weaknesses. This is equally true of the time you spend sitting in the reception office – you may be being watched! You have been warned.

Annabelle's Story

When I finished college I had an interview to join the Air Force. It was a weekend-long interview and covered just about all the different types of interview you could imagine. It started with a basic IQ test. This included some writing and some looking at pictures – that was quite stressful, but not too bad. After that there was an extensive medical examination to see if we were fit enough. Then we had group activities – they were really fun. We had to do things like roll a barrel across a plank without it falling off. Some of these exercises were done to highlight group co-operation, but then we each had to lead a group on a task. Next we were back in the classroom and had to work in groups of about six to solve a written problem.

'Up until then I had been having a great time. The other people applying were interesting and we all enjoyed it. After I got home though, I realised that I had really messed up the last bit. That was an observed group discussion. We were given a list of topics to discuss. I remember two were "Fox-hunting should be banned" and "Cannabis should be legalised". It didn't even occur to me to think what would be considered the official line on any of the topics, I just said what I thought. Looking back, I was so naïve that I can hardly believe it. I should have said what they wanted to hear. I didn't get accepted.

Chapter Checklist

Have you:

- ❏ **found out the nature of the interview?**
  - ➡ one-to-one
  - ➡ one-to-two
  - ➡ panel
  - ➡ group
  - ➡ informal

- ❏ **practised skills that are likely to be tested?**

- ❏ **investigated how long the interview will be?**

- ❏ **checked out how many interviewers there are?**

- ❏ **practised speaking to two or more people using appropriate eye contact?**

- ❏ **kept up to date with current issues in your chosen subject/work?**

- ❏ **thought about the attitudes your interviewers or group observers may be expecting to see?**

- ❏ **considered your views on issues relevant to the course/job, so that you have something to discuss?**

- ❏ **identified your own group behaviour in this type of situation, to decide whether it is positive or not?**

- ❏ **noted examples of relevant experience to discuss at any stage of the interview?**

- ❏ **considered how your educational qualifications will help in your application?**

8 The Unspoken Rules

You should read this chapter:

➻ about a week before the interview

By the end of this chapter you should know:

➻ the 'rules' of interviews for candidates
➻ the 'rules' of interviews for interviewers
➻ mistakes the interviewer might make, and how to overcome them
➻ how to make a good initial impression
➻ how to provide information if you are not asked the right questions
➻ how to cope with jargon and abbreviations
➻ how to deal with silence
➻ how to conduct a mock interview

Right at the beginning of this book we looked briefly at the format of the formal interview. Here it is again:

1 Welcome, sitting down, etc
2 Settling-in questions
3 Telling you about the organisation or college
4 Education questions
5 Experience questions
6 Your turn to ask questions
7 Interview finishes

The interview format

I have interviewed many people, for both jobs and college places. Whilst the other elements of the interview (discussion groups etc) vary quite a lot, the formal interview very rarely does. If you have been working your way through this book, you will have already prepared yourself for a good deal of the interview. Here are some more tips.

Rules for candidates

As you will already have gathered, candidates are expected to behave in a certain way during an interview. It is as if interviewing is a game and you have to play by the rules. However, it is true that many people, even those with wide experience, age and qualifications do not always follow these rules, and failure to do so can mean you lose the game. Here are some of the rules. Ignore them at your peril.

1 Be punctual
Better to sit around outside for half an hour waiting for your appointment than to make a bad impression before you start.

2 Be polite
Never, never be rude to ANYONE throughout the whole application and interview process. This is true even if someone does something so horrendous that you wouldn't touch the place with a bargepole. The world is a small place and you never know where people will turn up next. If someone does something unforgivable, like making a racist comment, and you feel you must do something about it, comment assertively and take up the matter with the dean of the college or the managing director after the interview. In this instance you may also choose to go to the Commission for Racial Equality or the Equal Opportunities Commission – more on that in chapter ten.

3 Never eat during an interview
If you're gasping and you're offered a drink, go for it, but it's really difficult to give convincing answers whilst you're munching a chocolate bourbon.

4 Never smoke during an interview

You need to be able to use your hands naturally to convey feelings. If the interviewer is a non-smoker you may be instantly crossed off their list.

5 Use appropriate body language

More on this in chapter nine.

6 Never complain about anyone

So your English teacher was useless and that's why you got a bad result, or you had to leave your job because you couldn't stand the idiot at the next desk. Don't say so. The interviewer won't be able to judge whether you're telling the truth or being vindictive.

7 Tell the truth

But you can be selective with it. Chapter one covers this in more detail.

8 Show you are interested in the job

Okay, so I've said that the interview is a two-way process, and so it is. You are here to find out about the job or college and you might not like what you hear. Never mind. Act as if you are genuinely interested. You might change your mind on the train going home, or you may want to apply for another course or job at the same place. If you behave as if you're not interested in them, why should they be interested in you next time?

9 Don't answer a question you don't understand

Ask for clarification. Simply ask something like 'Can I check I understand your question?' Then repeat what you understand the question to be. If you haven't a clue what the interviewer was on about, ask for it to be rephrased.

10 Check that you have said enough

Sometimes there may be a long pause after you have spoken. Details of how to handle this can be found later in this chapter.

11 Let the interviewer know if you have something in common

If it turns out the interviewer went to the same school as you, you can establish extra rapport by making a simple comment such as 'Was old Mr Jones there then?' Don't overdo it though.

12 Don't make comments on sensitive subjects

Don't mention these subjects unless you have to because of the nature of the course or job you are applying for. Sensitive subjects include:

- ➔ race (don't make racist remarks)
- ➔ gender (don't make sexist remarks)
- ➔ politics (theirs may be different)
- ➔ religion (ditto, or they may not believe in it)
- ➔ sex (well, you wouldn't, would you?)

13 Speak positively

Throw positive words into your answers, for example 'enjoy', 'enthusiastic'.

We look at EVERYTHING to do with the student so that we get a clear overall impression of them as a person. This includes personal things, such as home circumstances.

Quote from a college interviewer

Rules for interviewers

This is a heading you didn't expect, but it always helps to understand the other side's viewpoint. Delegates on selection/interviewing courses are taught all the following points.

1 Use open-ended questions
2 Encourage the candidate to feel at ease
3 Notice body language
4 Probe when an answer is unclear or fudged
5 Be objective
6 Probe gaps or irregularities in the application form or CV
7 Look at the candidate as a whole person, not just as a combination of skills and qualifications
8 Talk less than the interviewee – the ratio of speaking should be about 20:80
9 Set out the room so that there is no desk between interviewer and applicant
10 Have chairs of equal height and quality
11 Place chairs so that each can see and speak comfortably to the other
12 Look relaxed to help the applicant to feel the same

Great, except, of course, that not all interviewers have been on a course and some of them haven't a clue. Which leads us to the worst type of interviewer.

The poor interviewer

Now, if you think you're nervous about being interviewed, spare a thought for some interviewers. Often they are even more frightened than you, especially those people who haven't done much interviewing. This means that they are frightened AND clueless, which makes it tougher for you. So, what can go wrong and how can you get round it?

The interviewer talks non-stop
This happens surprisingly often. In one way it's a relief: it saves you the bother of speaking. The trouble is, you don't get a chance to sell yourself, and this type of interviewer is likely to take the last person they interview because they can't remember the others! All this means that you have

to make an impression somehow. There are a couple of things you can do.

1. Establish rapport with the interviewer by being encouraging non-verbally. For example, nod, say 'yes, you're right', 'good' and get the odd word in where you can. Remember to pick up on any points you have in common.

2. Even this sort of interviewer should ask you if you have any questions at the end of the interview. You can use this slot to provide any information about yourself that you weren't able to get across before.

The room is poorly laid out

There is little you can do about this, although it is acceptable to move your chair (a little) so that you can see the interviewer(s) more clearly. If you feel you have to do more than this, ask permission. Otherwise, you will seem to be invading the interviewer's territory.

The interviewer is aggressive

Some, though fortunately not many, interviewers use aggression as a ploy to see how you will cope under pressure. A variation is the 'good cop, bad cop' game, where one interviewer is nice and the other nasty. Keep your cool. Pretend not to notice the aggression. Respond to the questions in an assertive and calm manner.

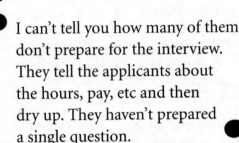

I can't tell you how many of them
don't prepare for the interview.
They tell the applicants about
the hours, pay, etc and then
dry up. They haven't prepared
a single question.

*Quote from a personnel officer who interviews
with senior managers*

The interviewer is disorganised

This can include:

- not having prepared for the interview
  The interviewer may not have read your application form, CV or Record of Achievement properly. They may not have prepared questions or know much about the job you are applying for.
- losing papers
  The interviewer may be distracted and distract you by losing objects, a train of thought, whatever.
- being late
  This is actually very common, especially if you are not the first interviewee of the day. Many interviewers fail to allow sufficient time between interviews and get behind schedule.
- allowing interruptions
  Unfortunately, some interviewers do not have the sense to divert their phones to stop callers.
- not following a smooth progression through the interview

They dart all over the place with questions. This person has not made an interview plan.

With all these difficulties, you will make a good impression by keeping calm, being reassuring, looking relaxed (so that the interviewer will copy you) and smiling encouragingly.

Andrew's Story

' I had an interview for nine o'clock in the morning for a job in social services. I had a million things to do before I left and it was a great rush, but I made it in time. I was shown into a grotty waiting room and there I sat for 40 minutes. No one explained what the delay was, although looking back on it, I think they were trying to decide how to run the interview.

'Eventually, I was called in and to my horror found it was a group interview. No one had warned me about that. I was introduced to all the people who worked in the team. What they didn't tell me was that one of the team members sitting there was applying for the job too. I realised something was odd though, when she kept taking the floor as topics were introduced.

'This group interview was followed by an individual interview which was nearly as badly prepared. The questions the interviewer asked were so wide, I didn't know where to start. Fortunately, I had the sense to keep asking questions in return like "Would you like me to talk about this...aspect?"

'The whole thing felt as if they were trying to catch us out, it was pretty unpleasant and I felt really angry. When they phoned to offer me the job I nearly turned it down. One of the first things I did when I started working there was to tell the manager how bad I thought the interview was. To my surprise she agreed, and even apologised. '

The interviewer knows less than you

This can happen if you have a particular area of expertise and are being interviewed by someone not directly involved in your type of work, a personnel manager for example. Likewise, some college lecturers interview for subjects other than their own. Never sound condescending if this happens. Remember, the interviewer may not be an expert in your field, but they probably are in their own. You can make the interviewer feel comfortable with their lack of knowledge by simply saying things like 'as you may know...'

The interviewer uses words you don't understand

Almost every type of work or course has its own abbreviations and jargon and many interviewers will unintentionally use them because they're so used to what is for them the short way of saying things. This means that sometimes you won't understand the question you are being asked. For example, someone applying for a job in a residential home for elderly people might be asked:

'How do you think we should treat EMI clients?'

Now, EMI is short for 'Elderly Mentally Infirm' but not a lot of people know that. Although perhaps you should have if you'd done your homework sufficiently. Don't panic! Simply say:

'That's not an abbreviation I'm familiar with, I'm afraid.'

The interviewer will explain and away you go.

If the interviewer uses a word you don't understand which is not jargon, see if you can make out the sense from the rest of the sentence. If you're still not sure, make a guess. Re-phrase the question and say:

'Can I just be sure I understand the question? Do you mean...?'

First impressions last

As has already been noted in this book, it is suggested that some interviewers make up their minds about a candidate within the first 90 seconds of the interview. Whether or not you are unfortunate enough to come across one of these interviewers, it is vital that your entrance is spot on.

In view of the fact that 90 seconds gives you little time to say much, clearly other factors are at work here. Firstly, there is body language. This is covered in more detail in chapter nine. However, below are a few pointers on making an entrance with suitable body language.

- Don't look apologetic. You've been invited to attend the interview and the interviewer(s) really want you there.
- If you're surprised by the layout of the room, try not to show it (some people do!).
- Look at, and smile at, all the people present.
- If you shake hands with anyone, shake hands with everyone. Let the interviewer take the initiative here.
- Sit calmly, don't slouch, but don't sit as if there's a poker in your back. It's a good idea to try to sit forward just slightly – it makes you look interested.
- If you have taken anything into the interview room with you, for example a briefcase, put it on the floor beside you, not on your knee.
- If you want to take brief notes, keep a smart notepad and pen to hand. Doing this can indeed make you look very professional. If you think the interviewer may feel threatened or uncomfortable about it, simply say 'Do you mind if I make a few notes about what you're telling me?'
- Don't put ANYTHING on the interviewer's desk. In animal terms it will be seen as a threat, an invasion of personal space.
- Don't forget your relaxation techniques.

Secondly, there is dress. If you have read previous chapters, you will have got this just right. If you haven't, you might like to go back and look at chapter five on practical preparation.

Candidates should always treat everyone in the room equally. On several occasions I have seen candidates assume that the women in the room were there to take notes and ignore them. They were actually other managers.

Quote from a manager in social services

Thirdly, there is that vague thing, rapport. We've already looked at this a little, but let's explore it in more detail. Experienced interviewers know that they have to be careful to avoid the two effects below.

- **'The nimbus effect'** – lovely name isn't it? Sounds like a science fiction book. In fact, it's when someone takes a dislike to you because you trigger some negative feeling in them. This will almost certainly be nothing to do with you, which makes it a bit tough. Perhaps you remind them of their rebellious teenager at home, or your accent takes them back to a bullying school teacher. There's not much you can do in this case. You can, however, lessen the likelihood of this happening by being especially careful about rule number 12 of the interview game: don't talk about sensitive subjects. If you make a glib remark about something the other person holds dear to their heart,

THE HALO EFFECT

you interact with interviewer

triggers a positive memory

interviewer notices only good points

has favourable impressions

increased chance of success

THE NIMBUS EFFECT

you interact with interviewer

triggers a dubious memory

interviewer notices only bad points

left with poor impression

decreased chances of success

you are going to have to work awfully hard to overcome their resistance to anything else you say.

Another small point: if you have been reading a newspaper on the way to the interview, keep it hidden. If its style or politics aren't the same as the interviewer's, it could trigger the nimbus effect!

●▸ **'The halo effect'** – this is the opposite. In this case the interviewer takes a liking to you because you have something in common or you remind them of their first love. You can sometimes tell this because you get warm feelings coming towards you, and the interviewer may make comments about whatever has triggered off their thoughts. You can bask in this goodwill without having to do anything except – don't blow it!

Lastly, there is your voice. Even in 90 seconds you'll have time to say a few words. Use those settling-in questions to test your voice in the room. A big room usually requires more projection of your voice, which is different from shouting. However, there is no hard and fast rule, except to try your voice in the room and attempt to pitch it correctly. If you are not sure how to do this, or if people have told you in the past that you have a quiet or loud voice, it would be a good idea to practise, with the help of a friend to listen, in rooms of different sizes.

If you are applying for a job or college place in another part of the country to your own, don't worry about accent, unless yours is so thick others can't understand you. Do, however, try not to use dialect words if possible because the interviewer may not know what you're talking about. Dialect words are those which have a meaning peculiar to a particular area. For example, children living in the south of England have 'pocket money'. Children in the north of England have 'spends'.

Coping with silence

We've already touched on this briefly and you should feel confident that your preparation will enable you to cope with every eventuality. However, sometimes it's not you who's the problem, it's them. There are a couple of reasons for this.

The interviewer is lost

We've already seen that interviewers are human and even the confident ones sometimes lose their thread. So one of the following may be going on.

- ➼ The interviewer is frantically trying to remember what you just said, their attention having wandered to tonight's dinner or whatever.
- ➼ The interviewer, being lost, is so distracted that your non-verbal messages to indicate that you have finished speaking have been missed (more on this in chapter nine).
- ➼ The interviewer is wondering what to ask next.
- ➼ The interviewer is wondering how to get you to tell

the truth in response to the awkward question.
- ➨ The interviewer is stunned into silence by your
  reply to the last question.

You haven't answered the question fully enough
Perhaps, you said only 'yes' or 'no' to the question. Or maybe you haven't picked up the body language telling you to continue. The interviewer should use probing questions here to get you to elaborate on your answers, but may fail to do so.

Whichever of these reasons is the case, you can be sure that at least some interviewers will be so sure of their own skills and expertise that they will assume that you are the problem, not them. In my experience, interviewing is like driving: no one thinks they are bad at it.

The good news is that both of these reasons can be coped with in the same way. Simply say 'Would you like me to add any more?' You have broken the silence, shown that you are a sensitive communicator and got them out of a hole!

 The interviewer showed me to my chair, sat opposite me and then said "Will you take the pens out of your top pocket please. I've got a thing about pens in top pockets." Phew! I didn't quite know how to react, whether it was a joke or not. It wasn't.

Quote from a man applying for a sales job

Something to add

As we saw in the chapter on questions and answers, it is usual for interviewers to ask at the end of the interview whether you have any questions. If you have been working through this book, you will have already considered this. But there is another use for this opportunity.

Sometimes, the interviewer does not ask the questions that allow you to say something you feel is important. Alternatively, you may feel that you did not answer an earlier question as well or as comprehensively as you would have liked. If this is the case, simply say something along the lines of:

> 'Before I ask you my questions, I wonder if I could go back to your question about...?' or

> 'Before I ask you my questions, could I tell you some ideas about what I might be able to offer the college/job?'

> I am impressed when people have a list of questions with them, it shows they've taken the whole thing seriously.
>
> *Quote from a college lecturer*

Making an exit

So, you've done a great job throughout the interview. Let's see how you can crown that achievement. Here are a few tips.

- smile at all the interviewers
- thank them for seeing you
- have a great parting line prepared:

'I'm sure that if you give me this job, you will be very satisfied with my work.'

'I'm sure that if you give me a place on the course, you won't be disappointed by my performance.'

- ↦ take the lead from the interviewer, shake hands if appropriate
- ↦ gather your bits and pieces tidily
- ↦ smile again and leave the room, closing the door gently but firmly behind you
- ↦ let out a sigh of relief and pat yourself on the back

There, not so bad was it? If you think the parting line is a bit over the top, think again. Say it honestly and sincerely – they'll love it!

The mock interview

If you feel unsure about interviews, then you need to rehearse. Don't overdo it or you'll sound stiff and unnatural. However, as already mentioned, the questions in the interview are likely to be phrased in a different way from those which you'll have practised. This will keep you on your toes and your answers fresh.

When we learn any new skill, including interviewing, we mentally pass through four stages. Let's use a driving analogy.

Stage one – unconsciously incompetent
Before people learn to drive a car, they don't go round all day worrying because they can't. They are unconsciously incompetent. They begin to have driving lessons and become:

Stage two – consciously incompetent
They now know that they don't know. They think things like 'Oh no, I've got to go round a roundabout. I'll never be able to indicate, change gear, and look in the mirror all at the same time!' This is the uncomfortable stage of learning. Fortunately, it doesn't last forever, but passes through to:

Stage three – consciously competent
Panic is pretty much controlled. A roundabout looms. The driver thinks calmly 'Indicate. Look in the mirror. Change gear.' They can follow the correct procedure but have to think about it. They are consciously competent. With further driving experience, this stage leads to:

Stage four – unconsciously competent
The driver arrives at the destination and thinks 'I don't remember a thing about that journey. I was too busy listening to what Jane was saying.' They have driven competently without thinking about it.

These stages are really useful to remember when you are practising your interview, or indeed anything else for that matter. They can help you to stop feeling bad when you're at stage two.

So, do a mock interview. Here are the steps to take.

1   Find someone who has some experience of being an interviewer and who will be able to give you some honest feedback.
2   In advance, give them:
     ➼ information about the job/college, which you received from the organisation
     ➼ the list of questions you don't want to be asked
3   Ask them to work out a list of questions they think you might be asked. If they don't know enough about your particular specialism, tell them what questions you expect.
4   Try to get the use of a video recorder. Set it up on a tripod or table, so that you can just leave it there, turn it on and forget about it. Don't forget to have it focused on you, not on the interviewer.
5   Wear your interview outfit so that you begin to feel comfortable in it and can see what it looks like to others.
6   Start the mock interview outside the door. Knock

and allow the 'interviewer' to let you in. Remember the halo and nimbus effects. You need to see what effect you have in the vital first moments.

7 Continue through the interview. Don't worry if you fluff a question. That's why you are rehearsing. Stop the tape. Think about how you can answer the question, start the tape and continue.

8 Do all the sections of the interview, including asking your questions at the end, and leaving the room after your brilliant final line.

9 Have a cup of tea.

10 Review the interview/tape with your 'interviewer'.

To give some structure to looking at the tape, or to discussing your interview if you haven't been able to record it, there is a format on the next couple of pages. If you can, get this photocopied and enlarged and have two copies done, one for each of you.

Before you discuss the interview, both make notes on how you think it went. This can be particularly helpful because we often have a false impression of our performance and you can literally compare notes.

Ask your interviewer to be specific. If they commented 'didn't look confident', ask for detailed information. What made you seem unconfident? Tone of voice? Hesitant answers? Body language? (If so, what body language?) You need answers you can use, so vague comments won't do.

Be a pain. Keep asking 'If that was good, what made it good so that I can do it again?' or 'If that wasn't right, what should I do differently to make it better?' Pin them down until you feel absolutely confident that you know what behaviour to change to improve your performance.

If you genuinely think the other person is wrong about some aspect of how you handled the interview, ask someone else to look at the tape, or practise the interview again with someone else. See if you get the same feedback.

Interviewing Skills Checklist

On the scale 1–10, please circle the number which you feel reflects how well the interviewee performed and then state what they did well or could do differently.

❑ **How appropriately was the interviewee dressed?**

1   2   3   4   5   6   7   8   9   10

What was good/could be changed? ....

....

....

❑ **How good was the interviewee's entrance?**

1   2   3   4   5   6   7   8   9   10

What was good/could be changed? ....

....

....

❑ **How well did the interviewee settle in the chair, remembering to put belongings aside/keep notebook to hand?**

1   2   3   4   5   6   7   8   9   10

What was good/could be changed? ....

....

....

❑ **Did the interviewee smile when settling down?**

1   2   3   4   5   6   7   8   9   10

What was good/could be changed? ....

....

❑ **Did the interviewee establish rapport quickly?**

1   2   3   4   5   6   7   8   9   10

What was good/could be changed? ....

....

❑ **Did the interviewee sell him/herself well, but without sounding boastful?**

1   2   3   4   5   6   7   8   9   10

What was good/could be changed? ....

....

❏ **Did the interviewee answer question 1 convincingly?**

1	2	3	4	5	6	7	8	9	10

What was good/could be changed? ....
....
....

❏ **Did the interviewee answer question 2 convincingly?**

1	2	3	4	5	6	7	8	9	10

What was good/could be changed? ....
....
....

❏ **Did the interviewee manage the right degree of friendliness?**

1	2	3	4	5	6	7	8	9	10

What was good/could be changed? ....
....
....

❏ **Did the interviewee ask appropriate questions at the end of the interview?**

1	2	3	4	5	6	7	8	9	10

What was good/could be changed? ....
....
....

❏ **Did the interviewee maintain appropriate eye contact?**

1	2	3	4	5	6	7	8	9	10

What was good/could be changed? ....
....

❏ **Did the interviewee use appropriate body language?**

1	2	3	4	5	6	7	8	9	10

What was good/could be changed? ....
....

❏ **Did the interviewee display any distracting mannerisms?**

1	2	3	4	5	6	7	8	9	10

What was good/could be changed? ....
....

❏ **Did the interviewee display knowledge of the organisation/college and current issues?**

1 2 3 4 5 6 7 8 9 10

What was good/could be changed?..
....
....

❏ **How well did the interviewee show enthusiasm?**

1 2 3 4 5 6 7 8 9 10

What was good/could be changed?..
....

❏ **Did the interviewee sound positive?**

1 2 3 4 5 6 7 8 9 10

What was good/could be changed?..
....

❏ **Did the interviewee have a great final line?**

1 2 3 4 5 6 7 8 9 10

What was good/could be changed?..
....

❏ **Did the interviewee make a good exit?**

1 2 3 4 5 6 7 8 9 10

What was good/could be changed?..
....

❏ **Was the interviewee's attitude positive?**

1 2 3 4 5 6 7 8 9 10

What was good/could be changed?..
....

❏ **General comments on interviewee's performance**
....
....
....
....
....
....

Chapter Checklist

Do you:

- ❏ know what to expect when you walk into the interview room?

- ❏ feel familiar with a typical interview structure?

- ❏ understand the unwritten rules of the interview for yourself and the interviewer(s)?

- ❏ feel ready for the unprepared or poor interviewer?

- ❏ feel confident that you can handle jargon and abbreviations?

- ❏ feel able to ask if you don't understand a question properly?

- ❏ know the first impression you make on people?

- ❏ feel comfortable with sitting down, placing your belongings tidily?

- ❏ feel able to manage silence effectively?

- ❏ know how to get in those good points about yourself that may not have arisen during questioning?

- ❏ know a great final line as you finish your interview?

- ❏ feel better informed now that you have done a mock interview?

9 Non-verbal Messages

You should read this chapter:

- ➦ two or three days prior to the interview

By the end of this chapter you should know:

- ➦ the importance of being consistent with your verbal and non-verbal communication
- ➦ typical body language signals
- ➦ how to look calm and composed
- ➦ how to 'read' the interviewer
- ➦ what signals tell the interviewer you have something to hide

It ain't what you say

Only about 25–35 per cent of the messages we give to people are transmitted through what we say. That means that about 65–75 per cent are given non-verbally.

One man came in and sat on his hands throughout the whole interview. Literally. At one stage when he became enthusiastic, he actually bounced up and down on his hands. I was working so hard at not laughing I had trouble concentrating on what he was saying.

Quote from an experienced interviewer

So here you are, with your questions and answers wonderfully prepared and you can still blow it. The good news is that most people display body language that is no problem at all, and you're probably one of those people. Nevertheless, trained interviewers will be on the lookout for what your non-verbals are saying, so you need to know what they are looking for.

One important point to keep in mind is that no one piece of body language should be taken in isolation, you need to look at the cluster of gestures to really assess what's going on in someone's mind. For this reason experienced interviewers will not interview with a desk between you and them – they'll want to be able to see the whole of you, right down to your toes! Why? Read on and all will be revealed.

Ethnic differences

The information in this chapter is based on white British body language. One of the difficulties about the whole subject is that it is said that there is only ONE piece of body language which is common to all people across the world, and that is raising your eyebrows very briefly when greeting someone. Therefore everything else is open to misinterpretation from one culture to another.

This means that you need to consider a few things. If you are not white British, but come from another ethnic group, but are likely to be interviewed by white British people, they may, in all innocence, misunderstand some of your non-verbals. Tricky. It certainly doesn't seem right that you should have to consider changing for other people. Sadly though, even trained interviewers cannot be versed in every alternative body gesture. Just to show you what I mean here are some examples.

> ➍ In some countries it is completely normal for candidates to show interviewers photos of their

families and, for example, to tell them how well their children are doing at school.

➡➡ Japanese women often hide a smile behind their hand.

➡➡ Some Mediterranean people are much more expressive with their hands than the British.

➡➡ American men are more likely than British men to cross their legs by putting one ankle on the other knee.

➡➡ Japanese people sometimes look at the other person's neck rather than eyes during conversation.

➡➡ In some countries women are considered to be behaving improperly if they look men in the eye.

➡➡ In some countries you beckon people with your hand palm up, in others with your hand palm down.

So, even though it's not right that you should have to consider your body language if you come from an ethnic minority, do remember the halo and nimbus effects. They occur even between people from the same culture and affect chances of success in interview. Also, no one, except perhaps Desmond Morris, who writes excellent books on the subject, can be an expert on all the varieties of non-verbal signals. If you think any of your body language may be misinterpreted across cultures, check it out with people you can trust. Once you've got the college place or job you can always set about educating people.

Giving the right impression

We've already discussed the fact that the clothes you wear say something about you, and this is indeed part of your non-verbal communication. Even if you dress from a jumble sale, you choose which clothes to spend 25p on.

The last chapter gave you a lot of tips on making a good entrance. Remember also to hold your head confidently, don't look down apologetically or passively, and walk with comfortable strides, not as if you're afraid of taking up too much space. Generally, look as if you feel good about yourself.

 When the other interviewers are asking their questions I like to sit back and watch the candidate's body language. You can learn a lot that way.

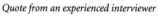

Quote from an experienced interviewer

Eye contact

A major factor in non-verbal communication is eye contact. If you've ever had a conversation with someone with a visual disability you may have found that the conversation did not feel comfortable, and there are good reasons for this.

Although eye contact seems so simple, in fact it's a highly complex and sophisticated set of movements that facilitate smooth conversations. What actually happens in a conversation is that we unconsciously pass messages to the other person about where we are in our speech by tone of voice and eye contact. Most people know these rules (albeit without realising it) and so know when it is their turn to speak. Here are a few points to remember.

- In white British society, it is acceptable to look people in the eye. However, too long a gaze can make the other person feel uncomfortable. Ever seen the actor Donald Pleasance? He gives you the shivers because he doesn't blink.
- The listener maintains more eye contact than the speaker. This eye contact, along with nods, 'mmms' and other gestures, encourages the speaker to continue.
- The speaker glances away whilst thinking of what to say next. This means that the speaker is alternately looking at the listener and looking elsewhere.
- Speakers who do not maintain enough eye contact can appear shifty, untrustworthy or lacking in confidence.
- Our pupils enlarge when we are interested in something or someone.
- Our pupils get smaller when we are angry.
- To establish good rapport, you should meet the other person's gaze about 60–70 per cent of the time.
- When you are looking at the other person, concentrate on the triangle between the eyes and mouth.
- If you want to make a point particularly strongly, concentrate on the triangle between the eyes and an imaginary spot on the forehead between the eyes.
- People who blink for longer than normal periods can give a message that they feel superior to the other person or are not interested in them.

‘

I interviewed one man who failed to make eye contact with me at all. He missed all my non-verbal clues telling him he'd answered the questions. He rambled on and on. I eventually had to tap my pen on the table before he got the hint.

’

Quote from a college lecturer

1. POOR CONTACT
2. OVER-CONFIDENT
3. MYSTERIOUS
4. CONFUSING

EXAMPLES OF INCORRECT EYE SIGNALS

Exercise

At an occasion when it would cause no unfortunate comebacks, perhaps with a friend, try using non-verbal gestures that are contradictory to what you are saying. For example, try talking about something you feel very enthusiastic and positive about whilst using nervous body language. What happens to the discussion? Ask the other person how they felt.

Arm gestures

The way you hold your arms when you sit gives away a lot about how you are feeling. Remember, if you display one of these gestures, the skilled interviewer should take your whole person into account, so don't worry if you suddenly become conscious of one particular aspect of your non-verbals and start to feel awkward.

Crossed arms
This can mean 'I feel cold', or, more likely in an interview situation, 'I feel defensive.' Probably the interviewer has made a statement or asked a question that you feel very uncomfortable about. If you see the interviewer sit with arms folded, think back over what you have just said. Have you upset the interviewer in some way? If so, can you retrieve the situation? Perhaps you could do something like show your palms, put your head to one side, or move your body sideways slightly and say 'Well, I suppose it depends how you look at it.' Open palms indicate honesty – try this gesture, you'll soon see what I mean.

Tucking your hands under the opposite arm pits
This shows that you feel superior, which is definitely not on during an interview.

Folded arms with the fists clenched
This shows definite hostility. Avoid doing this and watch for signs of it in the interviewer.

Handbag as a barrier
This is often used by women as an alternative to folding their arms. Do not sit with a bag on your knee during an interview. It is an even more obvious defensive gesture than folded arms.

Hands behind the head

This gesture, combined with slouching in the chair says 'I'm superior to you.' If this is combined with looking towards the ceiling, it effectively means that the other person can't get eye contact. It is sometimes used as a superiority gesture to stop the speaker being interrupted.

Open arms

This indicates an open approach. Arms are open when you hold them comfortably and loosely in your lap or on the sides of the chair. Open arms also make you look more approachable.

I interviewed this woman who sat throughout the whole interview with a big mock leather shopping bag on her knee. I almost had to look over the thing to see her.

Quote from a county council manager

Hand gestures

No, not the rude ones! You'd be amazed at how much the hands give away. Let's look at some of the more obvious hand movements.

Thumb-twiddling

I once did a mock interview with a man who twiddled his thumbs throughout the whole 15-minute interview. He wondered why he had been unsuccessful in getting a job after five years of trying. No wonder! He was giving very clear signals. They read 'You're a waste of space and I'm bored with the whole thing.'

Clenched hands
This may mean that you are simply relaxed, but can also mean that you are feeling frustrated or tense. It all depends on whether your fingers are held loosely or gripped tight, knuckles going white.

'Steepled' fingers.
Remember the children's game 'Here's the church, here's the steeple'? This is where steepled fingers are held either fingers up or fingers down and is usually combined with sitting back in the chair. Either way, it is often a gesture of superiority. During an interview, it is more likely that the interviewer will use it than you. Clearly, you want to look confident during an interview, but you must treat the interviewer as at least an equal. Definitely don't show that you feel superior in any way.

The other time this gesture is used is when someone is thinking before speaking. The cluster of body language you observe will tell you which is which, and will also tell the interviewer.

Rubbing hands together
This can be a sign of excitement. Alan Pease, in his book *Body Language* (Sheldon Press, 1988), points out that hands being rubbed together fast is seen as a sign that the other person will learn something to their advantage, whilst hands being rubbed together slowly is seen as a sign of the person being devious and dishonest. Lesson for you? If you're excited or enthusiastic about something you're talking about, as indeed you should be at some stage during the interview, make sure you don't rub your hands together slowly!

Hand-to-face and hand-to-head displays

Apart from eye contact, these are probably the most easily observed gestures, as people generally look at others' faces. And do they give away a lot!

Scratching the neck
This is usually a sign of uncertainty, and may mean that you are saying one thing whilst thinking another.

Hand in front of mouth
This can sometimes mean that you are lying. It's almost as though you half hope that the other person won't hear you properly and won't notice the porky.

Fiddling with your collar
This is usually a sign that you are feeling uncomfortable about something (getting hot under the collar?). The skilled interviewer would notice this and probe a bit deeper into whatever you were talking about.

Rubbing the back of your neck
This may mean that you feel you are having a hard time (a bit of a pain in the neck?). You may be having difficulty thinking of a good (honest) answer, or be feeling frustrated or angry about something.

Leg movements

This is where the interviewer really needs to have the desk out of the way or they'll certainly miss some interesting body language.

Crossed legs
Like other non-verbal signals, this should not be considered in isolation. Most people cross their legs simply to get comfortable or because they are cold. However, if crossed legs are combined with crossed arms and tense shoulders, they are likely to indicate displeasure. In an interview situation, this is likely to make you appear unfriendly and unapproachable.

A little story here. A man on a course I was running habitually sat not only with his shoulders tense, head down and arms crossed. He also managed to cross his legs to such an extent that his foot hooked on to the chair leg.

He wondered what he was doing wrong. 'My friends tell me I'm not sexy,' he complained. No wonder with such a clear 'keep away' message...

Crossing the ankles
This can indicate a defensive feeling. Again, the observant interviewer will notice this and probe deeper.

Fidgety feet
This can indicate impatience or boredom.

Mirroring

An interesting phenomenon this. When two people are getting along really well, they will frequently 'mirror' each other's body language, that is, both perform some act at the same time. The movement may not be exactly the same, but will be very similar.

HOW TO RECOGNISE 'MIRRORING' BEHAVIOUR

The following are examples.

→→ One person crosses their arms, the other puts their arms around a file they are holding.

- ► Both people lean forward at the same time.
- ► Both people scratch at the same time, but not necessarily the same place, and not each other!
- ► This is the best one. Next time you're in a pub just watch the people who take a swig from their drink at the same time. Now that you know this, you'll feel really self-conscious when you do it.

If the skilled interviewer notices that you are looking tense, they should help you to relax by sitting back comfortably in the chair and encouraging you to mirror their action. A poor interviewer will unconsciously mirror your tense body posture and the conversation will not flow smoothly. If your body language is positive and you happen to notice that the interviewer is mirroring you, it's a good sign.

Giveaway signs

'Giveaway signs' is a term used to describe an action that people perform when they are trying to cover up some feeling. Because most of us are fairly skilled at covering up our feelings with neutral facial expressions, it is as if the discomfort has to leak out wherever it can. This can be in a scratch, a fidget, a wriggle, a sigh, almost anything. The point is, you won't know you're doing it.

In the interview situation it won't tell the interviewer what you are trying to cover up, but will suggest that there is something about what is being discussed which needs looking into. Of course, the interviewer may be wrong. You may be thinking 'Where's the loo?' or 'Will I miss my last bus home?' but they are not to know that.

Irritating mannerisms

One thing you definitely need to avoid is distracting the interviewer(s) with irritating mannerisms. Not many people display these, but nerves being what they are, even the calmest of us can sometimes act in unusual ways.

Some examples of irritating mannerisms are:

- fiddling with jewellery
- twiddling hair
- clearing the throat often
- saying 'um' a lot
- fidgeting

Basically, though, they are any action which is performed too frequently. If you undertake the mock interview as suggested on page 125 you should be able to check out whether you need to take any corrective action.

Putting it all together

I expect by now you'll be terrified to move at all. You may think you're at the consciously incompetent stage. Well, actually, you're not incompetent, or probably not. Most people aren't. BUT, because many people are nervous during an interview situation, their body language may be more exaggerated than usual.

So, how does all this knowledge help? Well, remember the mock interview. What was your body language like? Do you recognise yourself from any of the descriptions above? Is there anything that needs correcting?   Do you have any irritating mannerisms that might annoy or distract the interviewer? If so, work on eliminating them. But don't, like the man in the quote, go so far as to sit on your hands throughout the whole interview. I expect someone had once told him that he gestured too much with his hands and so he was playing safe.

In fact, my experience is that people often use *less* obvious body language than normal during an interview because they're almost rigid with fear. A certain amount of stillness can convey a feeling of confidence, but a catatonic state makes it difficult for the interviewer to continue the conversation.

You need to think about your body language and find a happy medium between these two extremes.

Exercise

Next time you are in a public place watch people's body language without listening to what they are saying. What can you deduce about what is going on? Are the people friendly? excited? happy? threatening? miserable? in love? arguing? Watch for mirroring and giveaway signs. You'll find that you can tell quite a lot about situations without hearing a thing.

Chapter Checklist

Do you:

❏ walk confidently into the room, shoulders back, back straight, head comfortably centred on your neck, eyes alert?

❏ sit comfortably, but not over-confidently during interviews? This means holding your head up, not slouching, not putting your hands behind your head.

❏ put your belongings down in an unhurried way?

❏ use appropriate eye contact?
   ➼ make eye contact with all interviewers at the beginning of the interview?
   ➼ give main eye contact to the person asking the question, but glance at other interviewers from time to time?
   ➼ not look apologetic for taking up their time?

❏ maintain 'open' body language? Not sitting with arms *and* legs folded, but looking approachable.

❏ avoid giving away signs of your nervousness such as scratches, fidgets, finger tapping?

❏ note the interviewer(s) non-verbal responses towards you, and act accordingly?

❏ take into account the differences in body language across cultures?

❏ smile occasionally!

10 Equal Opportunities Issues

You should read this chapter:

→ a day or two before the interview

By the end of this chapter you should know:

→ what is meant by direct and indirect discrimination
→ when it is legal for employers to discriminate
→ who to contact if you feel you have been discriminated against
→ what to consider if you feel that the interviewer is asking discriminatory questions

It is sad but true that discrimination in employment is still a major factor in British life. This is despite changes in the law and efforts made by the Equal Opportunities Commission and the Commission for Racial Equality to balance the inequality as far as gender and race are concerned.

Of course, it would be easy to say that bias at interview was to blame for the fact that white British men hold a very high percentage of top jobs, but the picture is much more complicated than that. There are a number of factors at work that can explain the predominance of certain social groups in particular jobs. However, it has to be said that discrimination is one of them.

There are no laws at present to guard against discrimination on the grounds of age or disability. However, discrimination in selecting staff on the basis of race or gender is usually illegal in this country. The exception is when gender or race comprise a 'genuine occupational qualification'. Meaning? Well, the Race Relations Act 1976 says that being of a particular racial group is a Genuine Occupational Qualification (GOQ) for a job:

(a) Where the job involves participation in a dramatic performance or other entertainment in a capacity for which a person of the racial group in question is required for reasons of authenticity. An example might be the portrayal of a well-known historical figure in a play.

(b) Where the job involves participation as an artist's or photographic model in the production of a work of art, picture or film, for which a person of the racial group in question is required of reasons of authenticity...

(c) Where the job involves working in a place where food or drink is... provided to and consumed by members of the public or a section of the public in a particular setting for which, in that job, a person of the racial group in question is required for reasons of authenticity. A job as a waiter in a Chinese restaurant, for example, might satisfy this criterion.

(d) Where the jobholder provides persons of the racial group in question with personal services promoting their welfare and those services can most effectively be provided by a person of the same racial group.

The regulations concerning discrimination against one gender are similar. The Sex Discrimination Acts 1975 and 1986 state that

the circumstances in which a GOQ may apply are:

* a man or a woman is needed because of physical form, e.g. for a job as a model – or to be realistic, e.g. as an actor
* a man or woman is required to preserve decency or privacy, e.g. lavatory attendant

* the job is likely to involve the holder of the job doing his work, or living, in a private home and needs to be held by a man because objection might reasonably be taken to allowing a woman –

  (i) the degree of physical or social contact with a person living in the home, or
  (ii) the knowledge of intimate details of such a person's life, which is likely, because of the nature or circumstances of the job or of the home, to be allowed to, or available to, the holder of the job.

* the employee would have to 'live in' because of the nature and location of the establishment and there are no separate sleeping or toilet arrangements for men and women. In this case the employer must prove that 'living in' is necessary and that it would be unreasonable to expect the provision of separate facilities.

* the job is in a single-sex establishment, (or single-sex part of an establishment), which provides special care, supervision or attention, e.g. some jobs in a men's prison or single-sex psychiatric unit in a mixed hospital.

* the employee provides people with personal services promoting their welfare or education – which can be provided most effectively by a person of the same sex.

* part of the job is, or is likely to be, in a country whose laws and customs prevent women from doing the job effectively.

* the job is one of two to be held by a married couple.

(NB The sexist language is not mine!) The Armed Forces are not covered by the Sex Discriminations Acts, and there are special provisions for the police and prison officers.

Lorraine's Story

I went for a job as an admin assistant working for a major national employer. The interview didn't get off to a good start because the interviewers arrived one-and-a-half hours late! During that time I sat in the waiting room with three other candidates. When I was interviewed it was obvious they hadn't read my application form or CV from the questions they asked about my qualifications and experience. That was annoying enough, but worse was to come. My solicitor (who does some work for the organisation) had suggested that I apply for the job. The interviewers questioned me closely about my relationship with the solicitor, implying that we had something to cover up. I was livid. THEN, they asked me about my divorce, asked me how much maintenance I got, who would look after my small son whilst I was at work and whether I had a boyfriend now. I was so angry that I mostly answered with one word answers and a few times said "I don't see the relevance of that question," and refused to answer. On top of that they questioned me closely about my only criminal offence, which I'd mentioned on the application form. When I changed cars, I wasn't covered by insurance for a few days and got done for it. These three arrogant men said "We take this very seriously you know" as if I were a major criminal. I was so fed up with them by then that I said "Excuse me, I've been to court, been fined and paid my debt. I don't need to be tried again!" As I walked out of the office I thought to myself "I don't want that job". I wish though, that I'd had the courage to challenge them more than I did and looking back on it, I should have written a letter to someone in authority complaining about the interviewers' behaviour.

So, how do you know when you've been discriminated against? Well, there are three ways in which it is illegal to discriminate against people when selecting staff. These are:

1 In the arrangements that are made to decide who should be offered the job. This includes advertisements and instructions given to employment agencies. You do not have to actually be applying for the job to complain about this type of discrimination. For example, an advertisement says 'man required for...'.

2 In the terms of employment offered, holidays, sick pay, etc. For example, you are offered less holiday than Fred who's doing the same job as you.

3 By refusing to offer a person employment without legitimate reason.

To add to the confusion there are two types of discrimination. The first is direct discrimination. This is described by the Commission for Racial Equality in their booklet *A Guide for Employers* (CRE Publications, 1990) as:

> ...treating a person, on racial grounds, less favourably than others are or would be treated in the same circumstances. Segregating a person from others on racial grounds constitutes less favourable treatment.

Direct discrimination against one gender (usually women, but it could be men) is defined in the same way. Indirect discrimination, on the other hand is:

> applying a requirement or condition which, whether intentional or not, adversely affects a considerably larger proportion of one racial group than another and cannot be justified on non-racial grounds.

A racial group is a group defined by reference to colour, race, nationality – including citizenship – or ethnic or national origins. Race does not include religion. Jewish and Sikh people are usually considered to be members of racial rather than religious groups.

Again, indirect discrimination against one gender would be defined similarly. In practical terms, this means that employers must not discriminate, for example, against married women as opposed to single women, or against women with children as opposed to childless women. Nor should there be discrimination which makes assumptions about the types of things that women can and can't do. This means that interviewers should not ask questions like the following, some of which have been reported to the Equal Opportunities Commission:

'Are you engaged?'
'Marital status?'
'Do you live with parents or relatives?'
'Are your parents happily married?'
'Any plans to have a baby?'
'Are you on the pill?'
'How would you feel about working in an all-male office?'
'Do you have any period problems?'

I know, you don't believe that anyone would be so crass as to ask that last question, but they do.

If you think that you have been discriminated against at work, you can take the matter to an industrial tribunal.

For any further advice on sexual discrimination contact:

Equal Opportunities Commission
Overseas House
Quay Street
Manchester M3 3HN
Tel: 0161-833 9244

or for matters concerning racial discrimination contact:

Commission for Racial Equality
Head Office
Elliot House
11–12 Allington Street
London SW1 5RH
Tel: 0171-828 7022

To complain or not to complain

Your first instinct may be 'Of course I'm going to complain. I'm going to nail the so-and-so to the floor!' If someone makes a sexist or racist remark during an interview you've every right to be outraged, and I'm certainly not going to tell you otherwise. BUT, consider the following points:

- Was the person being *vindictively* or *unthinkingly* prejudiced? You may think it doesn't matter which, but it does. Someone who's vindictively prejudiced will give you a hard time if you have to deal with them in future. Someone who just makes a silly remark may be *relatively* harmless, in as much as they won't be out to get you.
- Do you really want the job or college place?
- If you do, will you have to deal much with the prejudiced person?
- If yes, do you think you can bear it?
- If yes, do you think you can change the person enough to feel you can cope?
- If no, can you bear to ignore the person?
- How much do you need the money?
- What risks are involved?

If you seriously want the place or job and can tolerate the person, think about not saying anything at the interview, but working on them from within the college or organisation.

If you definitely don't want the place or job, challenge the person, gather your belongings and leave the interview. Even so, don't be rude. Act firmly – you can get your point across just as effectively. You can simply say something like 'I find that remark offensive and discriminatory. I will stop this interview now and shall be contacting the Equal Opportunities Commission (or Commission for Racial Equality).'

Chapter Checklist

❑ This chapter has discussed discrimination in interviews. There are two different types of discrimination:
  1 direct discrimination
  2 indirect discrimination

❑ There are many ways in which you can be discriminated against. However, the two which are clearly covered by law are discrimination on the grounds of:
  1 ethnic origin
  2 gender

❑ In some cases it is legitimate for employers to state that they need to hire people of a particular gender or race. This is where race or gender is a Genuine Occupational Qualification and includes, for example, actors being needed to portray particular roles.

❑ Do you feel confident that you will know what to say if someone makes a discriminatory remark to you during an interview? Have you thought through the implications?

❑ If you believe you have been discriminated against, do you know what steps to take?

11 Tests for Selection

You should read this chapter:

- ↦ two or three days prior to the interview. If you have reason to believe that you may face intelligence tests, you may wish to read that section of the chapter earlier.

By the end of this chapter you should know:

- ↦ the range of tests you may face during an interview
- ↦ how it is possible to prepare for tests

School again

You probably thought when you left school or college 'Thank goodness, I'll never have to take another test!' Well, I'm afraid that tests are increasingly a part of everyday staff (and sometimes college) selection procedures. They provide the interviewer with another piece of the jigsaw puzzle that makes up a picture of you and your abilities. The tests are intended to provide a reliable and objective way of measuring your skills or some aspects of you as a person. Whilst some tests are well thought out, others can be less than objective and have some disadvantages. However, either way, you have to take the test if you want the place, so let's have a look at the type of tests you might encounter.

Skills tests

These have always been around. You want a job as a typist so they sit you in front of a typewriter to see how fast and accurate your typing is. Fair enough, you might be absolutely hopeless and this way the prospective employer can check your skills without great trouble or expense.

Other skills which might be tested are:

- shorthand
- strength
- driving
- machine-stitching
- teaching
- figurework
- spelling
- map-reading

So, if you're applying for a job that involves any of these, get practising!

Aptitude tests

There are six major aptitudes measured by these tests:

- clerical
- spatial
- manual dexterity
- verbal
- mechanical
- numerical

This means that, for example, to test your numerical skills, you may face numerical tests. For verbal skills, you may face a list of words and be asked to identify their meaning. For manual dexterity, your ability to do fine work (soldering, watch repair, etc) will be tested. Or for clerical work you may be given a list of sentences which are written wrong to sort out. (Get this one?)

There are a lot of these tests around, and if you are worried about them, the book list on pages 199–200 mentions a book that is worth looking at.

I was stunned when I was given a pile of newspapers and told to construct a tower. I didn't know where to start.

Quote from a student applying for a place on an occupational therapy course

Intelligence tests

Intelligence tests have received a lot of criticism over the years. There is always a debate about what intelligence is in the first place: the ability to pass exams? Common sense? Also, some tests have been found to favour white, middle-class people. Nonetheless, they are still used occasionally. If you think you might face one you can practise with a book called *Know Your Own I.Q.* written by H J Eysenck (Pelican, 1978). Mind you, if you can improve your scores with practice, do the tests really test intelligence or our ability to do intelligence tests?

Actually, most people seem to enjoy these tests, even if they can't always work out the answers. They are often similar to those found in quiz books and are certainly similar to those advertisements in magazines for Mensa.

Some of these questions are along the lines of:

What's next in this sequence?
A, B, D, G, ?

Insert one word that completes the words either side.
PEND (...) HILL

Some are little diagrams or pictures in a sequence. You have to draw the next one or find the odd one out.

Psychometric tests

These tests examine aspects of personality. However, that's easier said than done, because personality is so difficult to define. There are over 17,000 words in the English language that are associated with personality. In fact, the tests are really looking at traits, rather than making a judgment about personality.

Some people feel threatened by these tests because they think that the tester will be looking into their innermost soul. What the tester is looking for, remember, are your personality traits in relation to the job or college course. Even then, what they find is only true for you at the time you take the test. With age and experience, we all develop, and if you were to take the test again five years later the results may be quite different. Remember too, there is no right or wrong answer to these tests, so it's a little unfair to call them tests at all.

Psychometric tests examine a whole range of personality traits to check out whether you are:

- reserved
- mentally active
- shy
- trusting
- conservative (with a small c)
- relaxed
- stable
- confident
- reflective
- impulsive
- obsessive
- outgoing
- humorous
- venturesome
- suspicious
- happy to experiment
- tense
- autonomous
- happy
- risk-taking
- expressive
- susceptible to guilt

Tests of this type usually involve you answering a lot of questions in a short time. They are usually multiple choice. And not just the sort you got at school, but also questions like:

**Would you rather be
(a) an engineer or (b) an artist?**

**Do you like excitement?
(a) a lot (b) some (c) not at all**

**When I am in a big group, I like to take my share
of the limelight.
(a) yes (b) occasionally (c) no**

If you are asked to do this sort of test, you don't have much time to think about the answers, and this is deliberate. Some tests have 'lie' questions, which show whether you are trying (consciously or unconsciously) to make yourself look better or worse than you really are.

Also, they tend to ask the same question in several different ways to check the consistency of your answers. Unless you've got a brilliant memory for something you answered 30 questions ago and realise that you ought to make your answers match *and* you can do this all super-quick, it's not worth trying to fabricate your response.

In fact, if you believe that these tests have something to offer, it pays to be honest, because the tester and interviewer will know the type of person they need to do the job and if you don't fit the bill you'll probably either be unhappy in the job or not do it well.

A lot of people think these tests are dodgy, but I'm not so sure. My experience is that they can be very accurate indeed. Nonetheless, they only comprise one part of the selection process and very few organisations would rely on tests alone to choose between different applicants.

Team-role tests

One of my favourite tests in this category is the Belbin Team Role Questionnaire, which tests the type of role we take in a team. It shows, for example, whether we are good at fine detail, are the sort of person who comes up with bright ideas, are good at making other people feel good, or are a good leader.

When these tests were first devised, organisations got it a bit wrong. They tested people who were good at a particular type of work, then they tested everyone else who wanted to do that job. If they got scores that were similar to those already working well, they got the job. Unfortunately this led to teams of people who were too much alike. This meant that they didn't work well as a team. For example, it's no good having a team of people who all want to be the leader! Testers know now that for a team to work effectively it needs a mixture of team types. So, if they have a vacancy and they know they haven't got anyone who's good at, for example, fine detail, that's one of the things they'll be looking for.

Of course, if the testers have any sense, they won't tell you which team type they want so that you can't cheat on the questionnaire.

 We sometimes give people creativity tests. One of them is to see how well they can juggle with three balls.

Quote from a personnel manager of a large company

Graphology tests

Graphology tests look at aspects of your personality through an examination of your handwriting. If you see in an advertisement or job application form that you should apply in your own handwriting, this may be because the forms are being sent to a graphologist.

As with the personality tests, it is difficult to cheat at this. A skilled graphologist would probably know if you were trying to disguise your writing. You could get someone else to complete the form or write the letter for you, but what advantage would this be? Unless you know a lot about graphology yourself, you wouldn't know who to ask, even if you knew exactly what the graphologist had been asked to look for. They are certainly not just looking for neat handwriting.

In-tray tests

These are occasionally used to test the candidate's sense of priorities, logic and time management. They vary, but will usually include a list of items requiring attention. You have to decide in which order to deal with them. Here is one I use with people on a time-management course to test their skills in prioritising.

You arrive in your office early Tuesday afternoon, having been away from the office for the morning. The following greets you when you walk into your room. Place the items in order of priority.

1. A rep from ABC Ltd is waiting outside to see you about the order you placed for some new equipment. (Time needed for task 10 mins)
2. The head of department wishes to see you as soon as possible. (Time unknown)
3. The phone is ringing. (Time unknown)
4. You haven't eaten yet. (30 mins)
5. You have an urgent message on your desk telling you that there is a flood in the basement. You are requested to give advice immediately. (15 mins)
6. A piece of machinery has broken down. You are the only one who knows how to fix it. Three people can't get on with their work until it is mended. (15 mins)
7. Your secretary has a problem with some mail from yesterday. (5 mins)
8. Someone is sitting outside your door – you don't know who it is. (Time unknown)

9. The accounts manager wishes to see you in connection with the end-of-year accounts. (1 hour)

10. One of your staff is in the staff room, requesting permission to go home sick. (5 mins)

Tip: If you are asked to do this type of test, think about what is urgent and what is important. It makes the decision-making easier.

There is no 'right' answer to this type of test because you must make some assumptions. In this test, for example, you may be able to assume that you have a secretary to whom work can be delegated.

A suggested order for the test above might be:

(3.) You'll never be able to concentrate while the phone is ringing. But refuse to get into conversation, say you'll call back. Now the phone is free for you to attend to other matters.

(5.) Return the call about the flood in the basement and give advice over the phone. If necessary arrange to go down there.

(10.) Phone your secretary and ask her to tell the sick person to go home. This took 30 seconds instead of five minutes by not going to see the person.

(1.) Ask the secretary to tell the rep to come back in a couple of hours or to make another appointment.

(4.) Ask her also to get you a sandwich.

(2.) Ask her to phone the head of department to say you will be with her as soon as possible.

(8.) Ask her to find out what the person outside the door wants and make a decision based on the answer.

(6.) Fix the machinery, three people are being prevented from working while it's out of order.

(7.) See to the mail from yesterday with your secretary.

(9.) Arrange to see the accounts manager at 4 pm.

Testing and discrimination

If you think a test of any sort that you are given discriminates against you because of your gender or cultural background, and the latter may be particularly relevant if you are fairly new to living in Britain, you can contact one of the Commissions at the addresses in the previous chapter.

Feedback from tests

Many organisations now offer feedback after they have tested you and this can be extremely helpful. If you are not offered feedback, you could ask for it. Do so politely, don't demand. The feedback you get will help you to get a wider picture of yourself and your abilities. It may also indicate areas where you need to do some more work. Keep the notes on it in your interview file.

Chapter Checklist

There are many different types of test that you may face during an interview.

❏ **Can you remember the difference between those listed below?**

1 Psychometric tests	**5** Aptitude tests
2 Intelligence (IQ) tests	**6** Skills tests
3 Graphology tests	**7** In-tray tests
4 Personality tests	**8** Team-role tests

❏ **Do you feel familiar enough with the range of tests to stay calm when presented with one during an interview?**

❏ **Do you know what to do if you believe a test has discriminated against you because of your ethnic origin?**

3 After the Interview

12 Reviewing Your Performance and Looking Ahead

You should read this chapter:

- ➦ as soon as possible after the interview

By the end of this chapter you should know:

- ➦ how to review your performance
- ➦ what notes to make for future reference
- ➦ what to consider if you decide to write a follow-up letter
- ➦ what you need to do to update your interview file
- ➦ how to respond to a job or college offer
- ➦ what information a job offer should include

The show is over

Well, thank goodness, that's another interview over. You can relax and have a well-earned cup of coffee. But before you try to put the whole thing out of your mind until you hear the outcome, make some notes on your experience.

Okay, so you may get this job or college place and not need to reflect on your experience for a while. But unless you stay in one place for the rest of your life, you will need to do so at some stage. And I can tell you from working with people on courses that the most nervous are often those who haven't had an interview for years and have forgotten what to expect.

So spend a few minutes now. It can save you a lot of time later. On a piece of paper make notes on:

The journey
- ➦ Did you arrive on time?
- ➦ Did you arrive feeling calm?
- ➦ Would you have done anything differently with hindsight?

Your clothes
- ➜ Did they feel comfortable?
- ➜ Did they feel appropriate?

Your body language:
- ➜ Did it feel comfortable?
- ➜ Were you receiving good body language 'messages' back from the interviewers? If not, why not?
- ➜ Do you need to change any aspect of your non-verbal communication? If so, what? How will you go about it?

Your attitude
- ➜ Did you manage to sound enthusiastic and positive?
- ➜ Did you let the interviewer know that you had at least a fair number of the personal and professional qualities you thought they wanted?

The questions
- ➜ What were they? Write down every one you can remember. You may be asked them again in future.

●▸ Had you worked out in advance all the questions you were actually asked? If not, what can you learn from the ones you missed?

●▸ Did you do enough research?

●▸ Had you done enough preparation generally?

Your answers

●▸ Were you happy with them? If not, what would you change next time?

●▸ Were you pleased with the way you spoke?

Your questions at the end of the interview

●▸ Did they sound okay?

●▸ Have you thought of anything else that you would have liked to have asked?

Add-ons

●▸ Did you need to give the interviewer any additional information at the end of the interview? If so, were you happy with the way you gave the information? If not, what would you do differently in future?

Any tests, group discussions

●▸ Were you happy about how you did? If not, what could you have done differently?

●▸ Have you been offered feedback? If not, will you request it?

Follow-up letter

Sometimes, it can be worth considering whether to write to the interviewer(s) immediately after the interview. There is no hard and fast rule about this, I'm afraid. You will need to judge for yourself whether this will be seen in a positive light or not. Whilst it is done occasionally, it is not common practice in this country, and you may well choose to write only if you have something more you want to say.

Of course, it is not unusual for colleges to tell you on the spot whether you have a place or what grades they want from you, and many employers phone candidates the same night or next day with results. If, though, you have been told that there will be some delay before a decision is made, you might choose to write a brief letter.

---

14 March 1995

Ms G Sutcliffe
Kew Manufacturers Ltd
98 West Vale Street
Tyneford
Essex
RM1 2PG

Yasmin Singh
14 Lewis Way
Tyneford
Essex
RM1 2PG

Tel: 01961 35710

Dear Ms Sutcliffe

re: (name of vacancy)

Thank you for interviewing me today for the above post. I enjoyed meeting you and Mr Roberts.

I particularly appreciated the opportunity to look around your site and was very impressed by what I saw of your organisation. At the interview I omitted to mention that I have keyboard skills and thought you might like this information.

I feel very enthusiastic about the possibility of joining your company, as I feel sure that my previous experience and computer skills could make a positive contribution to the department and its targets.

I hope to speak to you again soon.

Yours sincerely

Yasmin Singh

Here are two advantages of such a letter.

●+ It keeps you in the mind of the interviewer(s) – a plus if a number of people are being interviewed.
●+ It provides an opportunity for you to say something you missed during the interview itself.

So you must decide. If you do write, keep the letter fairly brief and ensure that it is beautifully typed. It must sound positive and sincere. Start by thanking the interviewer for seeing you. Then let the interviewer know that you are still enthusiastic about the challenge the job presents, and that you look forward to being able to use your skills to good effect. Use positive words like 'enthusiastic' and 'enjoy'.

It is unlikely that many people would be irritated by a letter like this, but use your judgment when deciding whether to write one. You never know, it may be that the interviewer is having a tough time deciding between the candidates and your letter may just swing it.

The job offer

How job offers are handled varies enormously. Some organisations phone people the same day as the interview to tell them the result. Others write immediately. Still others write at some future date. It is perfectly okay to ask the interviewer at the end of your interview 'How soon can I expect to hear the result of this interview?' Generally they will tell you both the date and the method of contact.

So let's assume the organisation has decided to offer you that job you dreamed about. Congratulations! You will soon be taking the next step in your career!

You probably think that that is all there is to it. But in fact, before you accept *any* job, you should make sure:

●+ that you really want the job
●+ that you know (and are happy with) all the terms and conditions

The fact that you may get a phone call or a letter fairly soon after the interview means that you need to get your thinking cap on. Questions to ask yourself include:

- Do I really want *this* job?
- How do I feel about the people I met at interview? Would I feel comfortable working with them?
- Does the job have the career prospects I want?
- Am I happy with the amount of training that I will receive?
- Am I happy with the salary being offered?
- Is there anything else I need to know before making a decision?

There are also some things that you should check you are clear about before you formally accept the job. A job offer should include details of the:

- starting date
- salary
- place of work
- hours of work
- overtime arrangements (if any)
- holidays
- pension (if any)
- perks such as travel allowances (if any)
- sickness entitlement
- job title
- and JOB DESCRIPTION

You should have this information in writing before you accept the job.

Negotiating salary

Most aspects of a job offer are part of a fixed package, but the same is not always true of salary. What if you are not satisfied with what is being offered? At this stage in your career you probably can't be pushy, but there may be some leeway. Although some organisations have really strict grading systems (which means you will simply receive the same as anyone on the same level), others will make you a low offer to see if they can get away with it. They may be open to a spot of negotiation.

So if you think you're worth more than is being offered, you could say something like 'Well, I was hoping for £. . . '. Aim a little higher than you expect to get and then you can meet them halfway. Don't be offended if they don't budge to meet your figure. Perhaps they really don't have the money to spare, or they simply think that's all the job is worth (even if you are brilliant!). You will be able to tell pretty quickly if what you have been offered is the flat rate for the job.

Finally, if your offer arrives in a letter, you have the choice of whether to phone or write in reply. If you need any further information or want to negotiate terms, then it is probably more sensible to phone. It's quicker, and from the employer's point of view, if you decide not to accept the job they can offer it to their second choice without delay.

The acceptance letter

If you are happy with the terms and conditions in the job offer, a simple letter like this will be enough to accept.

---

21 January 1995

Ms D Weald   221 Overstone Road
Manager   Cambridge
Highsett's Ltd   CB9 8BB
12 High Street
Cambridge
CB1 1AA

Dear Ms Weald

Receptionist vacancy

Thank you for your letter of 19 January offering me
the position of Receptionist at Highsett's. I am very
pleased to accept your offer and agree to the terms
and conditions laid out in your letter.

I look forward to meeting you again at 9 am on
Monday 30 January.

Yours sincerely

Rachel Brown

University offers

You apply for most degree courses through UCAS. UCAS distributes your application form to the universities you have applied to. They also tell you each university's decision on whether to offer you a place or not (usually after you have been for an interview). The universities generally make you one of two kinds of offer:

- A conditional offer
- An unconditional offer.

1 A conditional offer

The conditions applying to this offer are that you pass certain exams at certain grades. This kind of offer is made when you apply prior to taking your examinations. If you meet the conditions specified when your results come out, the institution MUST give you a place.

2 An unconditional offer

This will make you feel good. An unconditional offer is just that – unconditional. The college is happy with you just as you are, with the qualifications you already have. This type of offer is usually made to people whose exam results are already known, or occasionally to mature students prior to their results being known.

Choosing your firm and insurance offer

When you have received all the offers that the universities are going to make you, you then have a choice. You must choose one offer as your 'firm' offer (or first choice) and another as an 'insurance' offer (or second choice). Your firm offer should be the university you really want to go to – if you make the grades for this offer, you will automatically be given a place there.

For your insurance offer it is sensible to choose a university that is asking for lower grades than your first choice. Then, if you don't do quite as well as expected, you may still make your second choice.

When your results come out

Once you know your results you can swing into action. Or should you? If you have achieved the grades requested by your first choice, you don't have to let them know – they will have been informed.

If you make your second offer but not your first . . .

If you make your second offer but not your first, you will certainly be given a place by your second choice. But if you only missed the grades your first choice were asking for by a narrow margin, it is worth you contacting them. They may still give you a place.

If you do not make either offer . . .
If you do not make either offer, it's definitely worth you phoning the institutions as soon as you have your results. Enthusing about how much you want to do *their* course or explaining why you missed that one grade might swing a decision in your favour. Equally, you may be in a year where many people failed to get their expected results, so you could still be lucky. But bear in mind that they may have many, many people phoning and they may need time to make decisions about people in your situation. Be patient if they ask you to wait and phone back a few days later.

If you contact the universities for any reason, remember to have your UCAS number to hand. It will save a lot of hassle and time.

What if you miss your offers and are rejected by both institutions?
If you miss both your offers and both universities turn you down, don't despair! There are systems designed to match students without places to courses with spaces. Scan the national newspapers and other media to find out which institutions still have places, and contact the ones you are interested in direct. At the time of writing, TELETEXT on Channel 4 gives the most up-to-date vacancy information in late summer.

You should also make use of the Clearing system operated by UCAS. If you have been applying to universities through UCAS but do not have a place on a course at this stage, you will automatically be sent a form.

Offers from colleges of further education

There is no uniform system for applying to colleges of further education. In most areas you apply directly to the colleges that you are interested in. In others you must submit a form through a central system to apply to any college in the region. Your school will be able to tell you how to apply to colleges in your area.

As with universities, it is normal to apply to more than one college. Most colleges will give you an interview, and will decide whether to make you an offer based on that and your predicted grades. If you have passed the interview, the offer you are made is usually the same as the requirement stated for the course in the college's prospectus. So you can use the prospectuses to guess how hard it is going to be to get into each college before you apply.

If your area does not have a centralised applications system, you can accept as many offers as you receive. When your results come out, you can take up the place with the college you prefer (out of the ones whose offers you have achieved!).

If you do not make the grades required by any of the colleges, it is still worth you going to talk to them. You may well still be accepted by one. You may simply be advised to start on a lower level of course, and to take up the course you applied for in six months' or a year's time.

Equally, if you just miss the offer for the college you really want to go to, you may still be accepted there if you are prepared to be flexible about courses.

Chapter Checklist

❏ **Have you made notes in your interview file on:**
- ➡ every question you were asked and how you answered them?
- ➡ how you would have preferred to answer any questions you were unhappy about?
- ➡ your journey?
- ➡ your interview outfit?
- ➡ your body language?
- ➡ what you noticed about the interviewer(s)' body language?
- ➡ questions you asked the interviewer(s)?
- ➡ your brilliant parting line?
- ➡ how the tests went?

❏ **Have you considered the need to write a follow-up letter?**

❏ **Are you clear about the difference between conditional and unconditional university and college offers, and how to respond to them?**

❏ **Do you know what you should check before you formally accept a job offer?**

❏ **Do you know what questions to ask yourself to check whether a job is right for you?**

13 Keeping Your Spirits Up

You should read this chapter:

➡ if you have not succeeded this time in getting the job or place you want

By the end of this chapter you should know:

➡ common feelings following a rejection
➡ how to write a follow-up letter if you decide to do so
➡ how to ask for feedback on your interview performance
➡ the dangers and opportunities you now face
➡ how to meet your basic needs
➡ ways to keep feeling positive
➡ how to set, and reach, realistic goals
➡ ways to increase your skills and experience
➡ points to consider if you are thinking of working for yourself

If at first you don't succeed . . .

This is the chapter I hope you won't need to read. In fact, I hope you will be writing a letter like the one overleaf.

But the reality is that everyone gets turned down for a job or college place during their lifetime, and probably several times.

> ## Remember
> There is no failure while you are still trying.

If this has happened to you, you may be feeling quite deflated. But remember, there are many people applying for every college place and even more people for every job. So, if you don't get offered another interview as quickly as you'd like, it may not be your fault.

---

15 May 1995

Mrs J Peterson
Personnel Manager
Davies Group Ltd
24 High Street
Walchford
Essex
RM4 9AZ

Jan Singh
22 Malta Road
Walchford
Essex
RM1 2BQ

Tel: 01213 46785

Dear Mrs Peterson

re: Vacancy for Clerical Assistant

Thank you for telephoning this morning to offer me the above vacancy. I am very pleased to accept and look forward to joining the Davies Group on Monday 22nd May at 9 am.

I look forward to meeting you again.

Yours sincerely

J A Singh

Common Reactions

It sometimes happens that people who are unemployed for a while experience a range of feelings. A lot of research has been done on this and there is a common pattern of feelings.

Shock

When you realise that you haven't got the job or college place, or have been made redundant, you experience shock. It is as if the mind can't take in what has happened. You feel a bit numb, as if it's happening to someone else. This is sometimes followed by:

Euphoria

Strange as it may seem, this is when you realise the opportunities opened up by what's happened (more on this later in this chapter).

Searching

This can be searching for another job, for reasons for failure, or for all the things you miss about what you had expected to happen.

Anger

You feel anger at whoever is responsible for not giving you the place. Or anger at your school or college for not giving you enough training. Perhaps also anger at yourself for not doing the interview as well as you would have liked. Occasionally this is followed by:

Guilt

Perhaps you feel guilty because you didn't do enough preparation or try hard enough in exams.

Depression

When you get really fed up, you can't be bothered to get out of bed. You feel there's no point to anything. Not everyone gets to this stage and you won't if you follow the advice in this book.

Gradual acceptance

This is when you begin to pick up again. You start making plans for the next interview or course or voluntary work. Life begins to feel okay again.

Acceptance

This is when you accept that you may have to wait a while for things to be exactly how you want, but are using your time well and are feeling happy with your life.

But, remember, not everyone has these feelings. It's worth knowing about them, though, just in case they hit you and you wonder if you're the only one to feel that way.

Moving on

So what can you do to avoid the feelings in the first place? The immediate and most helpful thing is to get some feedback on why you didn't get offered the place. It may be obvious, eg you didn't get good enough grades. On the other hand, it is not unusual for employers to leave people wondering why they weren't selected. So, ask.

The best time to ask, because your interview will be fresh in the interviewer's mind, is when they let you know the result of the interview. Often this will be over the phone. Simply say something like 'Oh, I am sorry. I would have enjoyed working at your company. I wonder, would you mind giving me some feedback on why I wasn't selected so that I can improve my chances in future?'

You have to accept that some interviewers won't want to tell you. If that's the case, you can't make them, but it's worth a try. Many will be happy to talk about it, if asked. I once insisted on giving an unsuccessful candidate some feedback, even though she didn't ask for it, because she needed it so badly and would never have got a job without doing some fairly drastic rethinking of the way she presented herself at interview (and I don't mean her clothes).

If you get a letter telling you that you have been unsuccessful, you can phone the interviewer to ask for feedback on your performance. When you speak to her or him, ask first if they have time for a few words because in a way you are asking for a favour.

Getting feedback serves several purposes.

- It tells you why you didn't get the job. This can be reassuring if, for example, there wasn't anything wrong with you, but someone else just happened to be better.
- If you are lacking in some way – eg interview technique, qualifications, experience – you can do something about it for the future.
- You are given another opportunity to speak to the interviewer. You may even want to ask if there are likely to be any other jobs coming up that you could apply for.
- You can use what you learn in a thank you letter.

My boss interviewed two people for a job. They were both equally good, but the job could only go to one of them. My boss phoned the "loser" first. The "loser" asked for feedback on why she didn't get the job, and she used the opportunity to sell herself. My boss ended up offering it to her instead.

Quote from an employee

Thank you letters

If you particularly liked the organisation you applied to for a job, but were unsuccessful in your interview, you may want to be considered for future vacancies. Some employers do hire people from their lists of people who have written to them 'on spec' or whom they know from elsewhere. The jobs these people are offered will not, of course, be advertised, so you won't know about them. It's worth, therefore, keeping yourself in the company's mind.

The letter need only be brief though it must be perfectly typed and presented. Here is an example.

---

14 February 1995

Mr J Dore	Julie Hirst
Personnel Manager	42 Epsom Drive
Hunters Engineering	Chelmsfield
Bloomfield Industrial Estate	Lancashire
Lancashire	RP2 5DF
RP1 8JQ	

Tel: 01623 48512

Dear Mr Dore

Thank you for speaking to me following my recent interview for the position of junior salesperson.

I understand that you felt that my experience was not quite wide enough for the vacancy we discussed, but I wanted to let you know that I was very impressed by Hunters Engineering and the work I saw being done. Therefore, if any further vacancies arise in my line of work, I would be very grateful if you would keep me in mind.

If you hear of any other companies requiring someone with my skills, I should be pleased if you would let me know.

Again, thank you for taking the time to speak to me. I hope that we will meet again in the future.

Yours sincerely

Julie Hurst

It is common sense to take a
method and try it. If it fails,
admit it frankly and try another.
But, above all, try something.

Franklin D Roosevelt

Dangers and opportunities

We've seen earlier in this book that some interviewers are, frankly, not very good, and it may have been your misfortune to come across one of these. Even if this is true, you should not feel over-confident, but should still carry out the exercise suggested in chapter twelve. A poor interviewer does not make you a perfect interviewee.

On the other hand, don't let it get you down. Remember, you still have a lot to offer. Come out from behind the sofa, and do something so that your chances are even better next time.

Everything you do in life carries with it dangers and opportunities. For example, if you had got the college place, you might have been bored stupid. Or the job you thought exciting may have been very stressful.

Here are some other dangers you may be thinking of.

1 There will never be another job (or college place) so right for you.
2 You may be unemployed for ages.
3 You'll lose face among your family and friends.
4 There may not be anything else for you to apply for.
5 You were awful and did a terrible interview.

Let's look at these items one by one.

1 There will never be another job or college place so right for you

Of course it feels like that at the moment, but only

because you haven't seen the jobs (college places) yet to be advertised. You may have to wait a while but it will happen.

2 You may be unemployed for ages
Perhaps. It happens sometimes, even to people with more experience and better qualifications than you. Later in this chapter we'll look at how you can use such time constructively.

3 You'll lose face among your family and friends
That's up to you. But this is my favourite saying:

Remember
No one can make you feel inferior unless you let them.

If you believe in yourself and your abilities, don't rise to teasing and use the time until your next interview improving your skills, people will soon see that your interview experience doesn't reflect your personality.

4 There may not be anything else for you to apply for
The reality is there may not be for a while, but eventually there will be. Later in this chapter we'll look at how to widen your choices.

5 You were awful and did a terrible interview
Is this true or are you being hard on yourself? If you really believe you did a poor interview, treat it as an opportunity to learn. Go through the exercise in chapter twelve looking carefully at all the points. You can make sure you never make the same mistakes again. More likely though, you weren't happy with just one or two parts of the interview. Again, learn from the experience.

> # **Remember**
> A refusal of a job or college place is not
> a personal rejection.

Exercise

Think of other dangers you may face. How will you overcome them? Keep your answers in your interview file.

Opportunities
But as well as dangers there are opportunities in your present situation. These include the chance to:

1 stay in bed longer in the morning
2 improve your exam results
3 not have to leave home and friends
4 look at other opportunities, now that the choice is not decided
5 brush up on your skills

Exercise

Think of any other opportunities you now have. Make a note of them in your interview file. Also note how you can make the most of these opportunities.

Opportunities are there to be used. Let's look at how you can use the ones outlined above.

1 Stay in bed longer in the morning
Actually, if you're unemployed, this is the last thing you should do. You have to set yourself a routine. People need routine. It can be flexible, but find one nevertheless. Get up at a reasonable time. Find at least one thing to do each day of the week: go to the library on Mondays; visit a

friend on Tuesdays; go shopping on Wednesdays; go to an evening class on Thursdays; go to the Jobcentre on Fridays, whatever. This will stop the days all blurring meaninglessly into each other.

2 Improve your exam results

Do you want to do the same exam again? Would you rather go for something just as suitable for your future career, but a little different? Would this motivate you more? How will you do the exams? What would be the best method of studying? Evening classes, a correspondence course, Open University, or studying alone? Work out the practicalities and get going.

It may be that exams are the least of your worries. Perhaps you need to brush up on your writing and number skills. If so, look for a local course. Your library will be able to advise you.

3 Not having to leave family and friends

Great, but remember you may have to do so at some stage, if the job or college you want is elsewhere. Do you need to do anything to help you feel more confident and independent? You could spend the time learning how to budget, how to cook, how to manage 'the system': banks, benefits, etc.

4 Look at other opportunities

Clearly, you had a particular type of work or course in mind, but many qualifications and skills can be used in a variety of ways. So step back and look objectively at yours. Are there other jobs or courses that will still enable you to follow roughly the line you want? It would be well worthwhile spending some time with your careers adviser, who will be able to tell you about the whole range of opportunities available. The careers office usually knows all about local job openings as well.

> When you get right down to the root of the meaning of the word "succeed", you find it simply means to follow through.
>
> *F W Nichol*

5 Improve your skills

You're probably thinking 'How can I improve my skills when I haven't got a job?'

No problem.

You can work for nothing! Okay, so you gain money from work, but it's not all you get. You also get:

- a routine
- self-esteem
- comradeship
- meaning to life
- job satisfaction
- a sense of purpose
- esteem from others
- personal development

➡ a reason to get out of bed
➡ professional development

You can get all of those from doing voluntary work...

Now, if I were going to interview someone who had been unemployed for a while, I would be very unimpressed if they'd spent their time doing nothing. If, on the other hand, they had used the time improving their education or doing some voluntary work, I'd look on them very favourably indeed. And there's no reason to think that I'm different from other interviewers.

By the way, if you are thinking of doing voluntary work, check with your local social security office whether it would affect your rights to any benefits. If so, is there some way round this? For example, by the people you are 'working' for agreeing that you could drop everything immediately if you were offered work?

What are the options for voluntary work and what can you get out of them? Well, the list is endless and beyond the space available here, but let me run through a few.

Working on a conservation project can give you a chance to:

➡ work as part of a team
➡ improve technical or practical skills
➡ learn about whatever the project is about
➡ prove yourself a reliable worker
➡ prove yourself to be punctual
➡ gain job satisfaction
➡ get real job satisfaction from improving the environment
➡ etc, etc. I'm sure you can think of more

Working in a children's nursery can give you a chance to:

➡ work as part of a team
➡ learn about children's development

- learn about how to manage children
- learn how to communicate with parents
- prove yourself to be a reliable worker
- prove yourself to be punctual
- enjoy the satisfaction of watching children grow and be happy
- have fun

Working in a charity shop can give you a chance to:

- work as part of a team
- show creativity in displaying products
- handle money
- learn selling skills
- gain job satisfaction from seeing your customers happy and making money for the charity
- prove yourself to be a reliable worker
- prove yourself to be punctual
- (perhaps) display good telephone manner
- learn customer-handling skills

Even if you're on the right
track, you'll get run over if you
just sit there.

Will Rogers

Working with elderly people in a day centre or residential home can give you a chance to:

- ➡ work as part of a team
- ➡ show creativity in providing activities
- ➡ show sensitivity in handling people
- ➡ use listening skills
- ➡ prove yourself to be reliable and punctual
- ➡ learn skills in handling people with some physical disability
- ➡ gain job satisfaction from making someone's life happier

Get the idea? The art is in selecting the right voluntary work for you. I expect at least one of the ideas above was a real turn-off for you. That's okay. Get out there and find out what's available, match some of it to your needs and away you go.

If you have a clear idea of the type of work you want to do, you can contact an organisation direct. If, though, you're not sure, try to contact a central organisation who can give advice on what's available. Your area may have a volunteer centre and the local library will have its exact name. Alternatively, contact your local social services department, under the county or borough council in your phone book. They may either use volunteers themselves or be able to tell you who does.

Working for nowt

Another idea is to offer to work for nothing to gain experience. Do you know someone who owns a business doing the sort of work you are interested in? Could they let you help out? There may be problems with issues such as insurance and safety, but it's worth asking. If they know you and your skills, you might get the next vacancy that comes up.

References

There is another great plus to doing voluntary work or working for free. You now have someone who can give you an up-to-date reference. That's very important because employers are only too aware that people who have been unemployed for a while or who have not had a job since leaving school can find it difficult to fit into a work routine. Also, you may have changed a lot in a few months and your old reference may not really tell an interviewer what you are like now.

Positive thinking

We have already looked at one aspect of positive thinking in the chapter on overcoming nerves. In that chapter I said that if you think positively when you go into an interview, you are more likely to do well. I'm pleased to say that it's the same with everything else.

Some time ago I got turned down for a job as a training officer in the organisation where I worked. This was a completely new type of work for me. Never one for negative thinking, I sat down and worked out a plan of action. Although I did the interview so badly that I cringe whenever I think of it, something positive came of the bad experience: I got my act together and really prepared for the next one.

First of all, I went to the interviewer and asked not only for feedback but, because I was an internal applicant, whether they thought I was a total waste of space or had really just been beaten by someone more suitable. Fortunately, it was the latter.

Next step. I went to the person who had got the job and asked if I could stand in for him occasionally, with my boss's permission. I also asked if I could do some small tasks on training courses to get my hand in. He agreed. I got the job when he left 15 months later. I believed I could do the job but knew I needed more experience. I went for it. I got it. If I hadn't, I'd have kept trying.

Of course, you can't do this if you're not in a job, but we've seen that you can get experience from voluntary work or by working free for someone you know.

Goal-setting

Think positive. Keep saying to yourself 'Even if it takes a while, I can do it!' Make a plan, set yourself goals.

Good goal-setting takes a bit of practice. If you make the goal too big – I want to be a brain surgeon but I've only got GCSE art – it feels completely overwhelming and you won't get started. So, if you have a big dream, a huge goal, break it into smaller steps. Remember that joke 'How do you eat a whole elephant?' 'One bite at a time!' To be a brain surgeon when you only have one GCSE your achievable goals would be:

- to get at least the minimum number of GCSEs
- to find out what the relevant A-levels or Highers are and where to do them
- to study hard and get them
- to find out about medical schools
- to get a place at medical school
- to qualify
- to gain experience
- to work up the career ladder
- to specialise in brain surgery

This involves quite a few years' work. So, the other thing you do is to set yourself rough target dates. If you don't do this, you won't get started or you'll let things slip.

Let's re-cap.

- ➻ Decide on your overall goal.
- ➻ Make your goal realistic. It's no good aiming for something that is impossible given your abilities and talents.
- ➻ Break down your big goal into smaller goals.
- ➻ Give yourself a rough timescale to achieve each goal.
- ➻ Work out what you need in the way of time, money, resources to achieve each stage.
- ➻ Work systematically through each stage.
- ➻ You're there!

It's important to write each goal, big and small, in a particular way. For example, you may have decided that one thing that holds you back is that you are very shy. So, would you write your goal as 'I will stop being shy within six months'? No, the trouble with a goal written in this way is that you won't know when you have reached it.

To keep yourself going and feeling bouncy and motivated, you need to be able to pat yourself on the back, and preferably get others to do so too. So, write down your goals in a way that means you can look at them and tick them off as you master them. 'I want to stop being shy' might become 'I want to be able to talk to people at a party without feeling nervous' or, of course, 'I want to do a job interview confidently'. Now you've got something you can measure.

Here are the steps you might use.

1 Join a club.
2 Keep in touch with friends. Phone them first sometimes.
3 Each time you know you're going to meet people, think beforehand what you can talk about. Read the papers. Keep up with what's in the news. Also, think about what's happening in the other person's

life so that you can talk about that.

4 Practise being a good listener. Ask for feedback from a friend on whether you have achieved this.

5 Practise some positive self-talk.

6 Read a book on improving self-confidence.

That's a lot of steps, but you'll get the idea. You can actually tick off each of these items as you achieve them. This will be terrific for your self-confidence.

Each of these steps is measurable. As you take these actions, you can measure how well you do them. Other ways of measuring achievements are:

Percentages 'I will read 10 per cent of this book each day.'

Frequency of something happening 'I will not take more than one day a week off from studying.'

Time limits 'I will find and join a club within the next month.'

Absolute bans 'I will not sit here for hours when I feel low. I'll go for a walk or visit a friend.'

It's a very good idea to talk about your goals to a friend or relation you can trust. Don't tell anyone who will try to put you off. Ask whoever you choose to help you in whatever way you need. Perhaps to notice when you do things well; to let you know what you can do differently; to keep you going when you get disheartened.

Working for yourself

Working for yourself can seem an attractive idea if you can't get the job or college place you want. But it is no easy option. Ask any successful business owner and they will tell you they work long hours, take few holidays and have a lot of worries. Even people whose businesses are established can't relax. A recession can put paid to all their years of hard work. On top of that, if your business idea involves borrowing money, and most of them do, you will find that difficult in itself, especially if you have no security, such as a house, behind you.

There is a lot to think about before you decide to go into business. This checklist may help you to think through the issues.

Yes No Item

❏ ❏ Do you have a product or service that people want to buy?

❏ ❏ Are you dedicated enough to put in a lot of time and effort?

❏ ❏ Can you stand the strain and worry of trying to get yourself established?

❏ ❏ Can you live with the uncertainty of not knowing when money will come in?

❏ ❏ Can you cope with several things at the same time?

❏ ❏ Do you usually see things through to the end or give up halfway?

❏ ❏ Are your decisions usually good ones?

❏ ❏ Can you chase debtors for money?

❏ ❏ Can you raise the money?

❏ ❏ Can you sell your product or services?

❏ ❏ Can you cope with the loneliness of being self-employed?

❏ ❏ Are you well organised?

❏ ❏ Can you cope with a lot of paperwork?

❏ ❏ Can you keep accurate records of your work and finances?

❏ ❏ Can you deal confidently with banks, suppliers, tax officers, etc?

❏ ❏ Will you get support from your family and friends?

❏ ❏ Do you have any big debts?

❏ ❏ Are you good at selling?

If the answer is 'yes' to most of these questions and you decide to go for it, you may still need help.

Training and Enterprise Councils, and LECs in Scotland
Each area of Great Britain has a training and enterprise council or local enterprise company in Scotland, which is an agency established to help businesses. Part of its work is helping people to start their own businesses. Each of the 82 TECs and 22 LECs is run independently and this means that each offers a different service, so it is not possible for me to give details of what may be on offer in your area.

However, the help they are able to give may include:

- grants to give you an income for a certain period while you get going (you have to be 18 to get a grant)
- advice from an experienced business counsellor
- training courses, which are free in some areas, on different aspects of starting and running a business
- helpful booklets
- a freephone hotline for advice (some areas)
- advice on other training courses in the subjects you want

So it's a good idea to give them a ring before you start. They can show you the pitfalls before you trip into them.

Above all, plan, plan, plan. A lot of people make a success of their business, but a lot fail too, sometimes leaving themselves with enormous debts that plague them for years. So think very carefully before you set out on this course of action.

Chapter Checklist

Do you feel you understand:

- ❏ how to get feedback from the interviewer?

- ❏ how to write a follow-up letter?

- ❏ the feelings you may experience as a result of being unemployed for a while?

- ❏ the dangers you may face as a result of your 'rejection' and how to face or overcome them?

- ❏ the opportunities you have now and how to use them?

- ❏ how to improve your skills through voluntary work?

- ❏ how to set goals for yourself?

- ❏ what you need to consider if you decide to work for yourself?

- ❏ where to go for help if you decide to set up in business on your own?

14 Further Information and Book List

The following are good sources of information for research into companies and current issues.

Dun & Bradstreet Guide to Key British Enterprises Gives a wealth of information on major companies, from turnover to names of key people. Your local library should be able to help you find this book.

Training and Enterprise Councils (TECs) or Local Enterprise Companies (LECs) These organisations are regionally based and you can find their number in your local phone book. Alternatively, there is a freephone number 0800 222 999.

Chambers of Trade or Chamber of Commerce, Trade and Industry Again, regional offices can be tracked down through your phone book.

Kelly's Business Directory has information on companies based in the UK. Look in your local library for this book.

Stock Exchange Yearbook has financial information on all quoted public companies. Your library should have a copy of this yearbook.

UK Kompass Register (Kompass Publishers) Two volumes are published each year. One provides information on products and services and the other gives information on areas such as activities, staffing, directors. You should be able to find a copy of this in your local library.

Times 1000 Leading Companies (Times Newspapers Ltd) Information on all major firms. Also details organisations that offer management and other training courses.

National Press Even if the national press is unlikely to be writing about the organisation you are applying to, it is worth keeping an eye on the papers from the time you are invited to interview (or earlier) so that you are aware of relevant current issues.

Trade/Professional Journals or Magazines Again, your library will be able to help you to locate these.

Local Press Keep an eye out for what is going on in your area. This will be particularly important for smaller companies, which will be difficult to research using any of the methods suggested above.

Careers Office Your local careers office is a mine of information. They may well know about the organisation you are interested in.

Asking Around Try to track down people who know the organisation you're interested in. Learn about it from the horse's mouth!

Book List

You may find these books helpful to your interview preparation.

How to Interview and be Interviewed
by M Brown and G Brandreth, Sheldon Press 1986

Know Your Own I.Q.
Hans J Eysenck, Pelican 1990

Know Your Own Personality
Hans J Eysenck & Wilson, Penguin 1991

How to Pass that Interview
J Johnstone, How To Books 1991

Who's Hiring Who?
R Lathrop, Ten Speed Press 1989

The Pocket Guide to Manwatching
Desmond Morris, Triad Grafton 1987

Body Language
A Pease, Sheldon Press 1992

The Interview Game
C Roberts, BBC Publications 1986

Great Answers to Tough Interview Questions
Martin J Yate, Kogan Page 1992